I Had A Secret
For Seventeen Years

I Had A Secret
For Seventeen Years

A Story of Redemption and Healing after Abortion

Tori Shaw

Foreword by Angela Forker

RESOURCE *Publications* · Eugene, Oregon

I HAD A SECRET FOR SEVENTEEN YEARS
A Story of Redemption and Healing after Abortion

Resource Publications
An Imprint of Wipf and Stock Publishers
199 W. 8th Ave., Suite 3
Eugene, OR 97401

www.wipfandstock.com

PAPERBACK ISBN: 978-1-7252-7140-1
HARDCOVER ISBN: 978-1-7252-7139-5
EBOOK ISBN: 978-1-7252-7141-8

Manufactured in the U.S.A.   07/07/20

For Taylor,
God is using our story, sweet girl. I love you.

For Bryan,
Our path has been rocky at times but there is no one else I'd rather
journey through this life with. I love you more than words can say.
Thank you for allowing me to share our story so that God may use it
for His glory and the good of others.

For Angelique Krawczynski,
Thank you for the countless hours you spent editing this book. God
could not have blessed me with a more perfect editor and friend.

For post-abortive women everywhere,
Hiding often feels like the safest choice, but God desires so much more
for you. It's time to step out from the shadows of your secret and into
the light. Freedom awaits.

Contents

Author's Note

THE MEMORIES CONTAINED WITHIN these pages are just that, memories. The stories and situations from my life are written as I recall them. Within the pages of this book, I will share with you how *I* felt and the impact these events had on *my* life. My prayer is that no one will be hurt by my memories but will understand that each one of these situations has been used by our Mighty God. He has used them to transform me into the person I am today. The purpose of sharing my story is to show how God can use *anything* for good in the lives of those who love Him. (Romans 8:2)

My one request, as I invite you into my life, is for you to read the book in its entirety. Reading bits and pieces of my story may leave you feeling hopeless, angry, or disappointed. Reading the story from cover to cover, however, will prove that not even one difficult situation has been wasted. God has given back all that was stolen, and more. (Joel 2:25–26, Isaiah 61:7)

There have been many tears shed while writing this book, both painful and joyful. This process has been therapeutic for me, in many ways, but it's also an honor to share all that God has done for me and through the story I tried so desperately to hide for seventeen years. I have already prayed for each of you, that God might use my transparency to infuse you with hope and enable you to trust His plan for your life. There is not one thing that can separate you from the love of God. (Romans 8:31) God never looks at you with disgust or aggravation. No matter what you've done or where you've been, He loves you and has beautiful plans for you; plans that He designed before you were even born. (Jeremiah 1:5) He is not mad at you and is not punishing you for your choices. (Romans 8:1) Even the ugliest parts of our past are like putty with purpose in His mighty and powerful hands. When we allow Him to, He will bring beauty from our brokenness and transform our past into our purpose.

Author's Note

"What was intended to harm me, God intended for good to accomplish what is now being done, the saving of many lives."(Genesis 50:20)

By His Grace,
Tori

Foreword

THE FIRST TIME TORI reached out to me, she contacted me about being a part of my "After the Abortion" photography series. Her story touched my heart and I felt it could help other post-abortive men and women on their journey toward healing.

As we communicated, Tori told me how she was able to face her fears and actually go inside the former abortion clinic where she had her abortion two decades ago. She explained that it was now a beauty school. When she had returned to it a couple of months before, she made a memorial to her baby outside the back door of the former clinic.

When we began to plan her photography session, Tori expressed a desire to do her session inside the former abortion clinic. The more I thought about it, the more I felt we needed to do it there. Amazingly, everything fell into place and I found myself with Tori at the very location where her secret began. As we got out of the car and I grabbed my camera, I was overcome by a feeling of darkness and heaviness. Tori agreed that she felt it, too. I have never felt such evil. It's a feeling I will never forget!

I was so proud of Tori, as she not only faced her past, but she continued on with our plan, even though the feeling of oppression was so strong the entire time we were on that property. As we walked through the halls and went through the different rooms to see which spots would work best for our shoot, I noticed that the heaviness grew as we got closer to the back of the building. Tori pointed out that the abortions were performed there. When we got to the back door, the feeling was the strongest. Tori shared that the babies' remains were tossed in bins outside that door. It was quite significant that Tori chose that spot to make a memorial for her baby.

Throughout our entire session, Tori showed great courage. She was willing to don a hospital gown for most of the photos. (I felt that would make her photos especially impactful.) She willingly reenacted painful memories and was even willing to squeeze under the counter where the babies' remains were pieced back together, all for the sake of helping prevent just one person from suffering the pain she went through after her abortion!

After her session, she brought me to her ministry building. I was so pleased to see the beauty that is happening through her life. Beauty that was all birthed out of her pain and suffering once she was willing to bravely share her secret with the world. Tori is an extraordinary woman who has given her past to God and is allowing Him to use it for His glory. I was very honored that Tori would want to be a part of the "After the Abortion" photography series and share her story with the world through my photos. I was happier yet, to hear that she would be sharing her story through this book. I am sure you will be moved by it and by her beautiful heart!

Angela Forker

1

Waking Up in a Nightmare

I SLOWLY OPENED MY heavy eyes. *"Where am I?"* I thought. I looked around slowly. I saw sterile white walls, a little white board with a nurse's name scribbled on it, and a large window covered in blinds. I noticed I was lying in a hospital bed covered in flimsy white blankets. The bars along the side kept me from falling out and allowed me to adjust my position as well. To my right stood a tall two-hook-IV stand. To my left was an empty blue chair with a bag for personal belongings. In my groggy state I realized, I was in a hospital room and I was the patient.

My mind began to blur. I tried to put memories together as if they were a puzzle. *"Wasn't all of that a dream?"* I asked myself desperately. *"Why am I laying here? Why am I hooked up to this IV?"* My mind was groggy, probably because of the IV. I scanned the room and observed that no one was there with me. I was utterly alone and had a long list of questions. I could not ask even one of them. Shame seeped into my heart as I realized, I didn't want to ask anyone. I was beginning to realize, what I thought had been my worst nightmare, wasn't a dream at all.

It was hard to think clearly but I searched my memory for clues to exactly what was happening. I remembered being sick for the past couple of weeks, not knowing why I kept throwing up. The first time I had gotten sick to my stomach I had been eating lunch with my boyfriend, Bryan. I couldn't eat my food and ended up getting sick numerous times in the restaurant's bathroom. After our lunch, Bryan took me home and I went to bed, believing I had a stomach bug of some sort. Over the next couple of weeks, I experienced a few sporadic days of feeling pretty good. Good enough, at least, to go back to work at my summer job. I was the two-year-old class assistant at a children's center. At sixteen years old, I was now assisting in a classroom I once played in. I loved children and this was the perfect way to make extra money during the summer before my senior year of high school.

Even though I wasn't feeling up to it, I went back to work and cared for the most precious two-year-olds. One afternoon, as I walked down the hall, I had to rush into the bathroom, hoping I would make it to the toilet. I was sick again. I quickly realized I needed to go home. I knew I had to tell the director of the center I was sick, but I was so nervous. I had already missed several days of work because of this stomach bug. *Would she be angry with me? Would she fire me?* I didn't know, but somehow, I had to find the energy to talk with her.

I slowly entered her office and sat in a wooden chair with stiff black cushions in front of her desk. I shared my current state with her, and it seemed obvious she knew I wasn't lying. She understood that going home would be best for me but made sure to let me know that I couldn't keep missing work. I left her office feeling like such a disappointment. That was just the beginning of that overwhelming emotion.

I went home, laid in bed, and did not get up again. My mom lovingly placed a trash can beside my bed and laid a beach towel along the bedside so I wouldn't ruin my sheets. I repeatedly threw up, even though there was nothing in my stomach. I was so exhausted. I couldn't keep my eyes open long enough to watch a TV show or take a sip of my soda. I remember forcing myself to change positions in the bed. I flipped over onto my belly but realized my abdomen was very sore. So, I slept on my side and back for what seemed like days. I don't recall how long I slept, only waking to get sick in the can beside my bed.

My mom and stepdad checked on me often. One evening they entered my room and had a look of deep concern on their faces. My stepdad wanted to take me to the emergency room, but I begged to stay home. I was too tired and weak to go. They agreed that I could stay in the bed if I would allow my mom to take me to the pediatrician in the morning. I accepted. I probably would have accepted any deal, as long as I didn't have to get up right then.

When the morning arrived, my mom woke me with the reminder that we were heading to the doctor's office. She had made an appointment for me and I needed to get dressed. I scrounged around my room, found my favorite gray sweatpants and an old t-shirt. As I slowly got dressed, I could tell my waist was smaller. I found a pair of black flip flops, threw my hair in a ponytail, and made my way down the stairs.

Laying in the hospital bed, I tried to remember more. *What happened in the doctor's office?* Clearing my mind, filtering through the fog the medication was causing, my next memory surfaced.

I had been laying on a silver bed covered by a white paper sheet. The bed was propped up some because, as I told the doctor, I felt more nauseous when I laid flat on my back. She asked a few questions such as, "Are you allergic to any foods?" "Do you know if you're allergic to any medications? "When was your last period?" My mind rushed back over the past month. "I had my period about three weeks ago," I said. She did a physical exam, then pressed on my stomach and I began to squirm. She mentioned something about Appendicitis or Gastroenteritis. I didn't care what it was, I just wanted someone to help me feel better!

The door creaked as it opened, and a young blonde nurse stuck her head inside the door. Her look beckoned the doctor and she asked a coded question in a secretive voice, "Did you want to do any other tests?" The doctor looked puzzled and said, "No, I think we did all of the tests we need." The nurse was visibly annoyed and motioned towards the doctor. "Can you just come out here for a moment," she asked. The doctor left the room and reentered with the look of shock on her face.

Fear suddenly engulfed me. *What was wrong with me? Why wasn't she hiding her look of shock from me?* She slowly walked toward me and took my hand. Her quiet voice began to speak but my ears could only hear a muffled mummering. My voice was shaky, but I was able to ask, "What did you say?" She repeated the words no sixteen-year-old girl ever wants to hear. "Tori," she said, "you're pregnant."

"What?" I yelled out. "I can't be. I had my period. Remember, I just told you. It wasn't that long ago. I thought you couldn't have a period if you're pregnant." My mind was racing. I could feel my heart pounding wildly in my chest. "Most women do not have a period when they get pregnant. Do you remember if your period was normal? Did it come at the correct time? Was it heavy or light?" she asked.

I tried desperately to remember exactly what it had been like, as if it would change the results of the test. "I don't know. It may have been lighter than usual, yea I think it was. But I thought you couldn't have any period at all if you were pregnant." I replied. She looked at me with such sadness. She could tell how scared I was and that the possibility of being pregnant had not even crossed my mind. "Most women do not have any bleeding when they are pregnant, but some have a little spotting at the beginning of their pregnancies as the embryo implants itself along the uterine wall. Sometimes, the bleeding can be significant enough to appear as a very light period. I'm guessing that is what happened with you," she said softly.

I began to cry as the news settled into my mind and I attempted to make sense of her words. *I guess I hadn't had my period.* As a sixteen-year-old girl who had only been menstruating for a couple of years, I had assumed any blood meant you were menstruating as normal. I was so naïve.

I was struck with fear and began to cry loudly. My mom had been sitting in the waiting area but entered the exam room when she heard me screaming. She was so concerned for me and asked me what was wrong. She looked back and forth, giving her attention to the doctor and to me. For the first time, I had to say the words out loud. "Mom, I'm pregnant." She hugged me as her tears flowed. She said, "I wondered if that was the problem. I was sick like that when I was pregnant with you and with your brother."

My mind couldn't calm down. *How could I have let this happen? What would Bryan say? Why hadn't my mom told me she suspected I was pregnant? Is this why I couldn't lay on my belly without pain? Or lay flat on my back without throwing up? When did this happen? What was I going to do? Everyone will hate me. This will ruin my life. This is my worst nightmare. It's probably my mom's worst nightmare too. Everyone will judge me; they'll call me a slut. I knew I shouldn't have sex before marriage, but I didn't have the self-control to say no. This is what I get. This is what I deserve.*

My unruly thoughts were interrupted by the doctor's voice. I could barely focus on her words. Instead, my eyes were glued to her swollen belly. I hadn't even realized it. That very doctor, the one that had given me such horrific news, was about eight months pregnant. There was no mistaking it. She would have a baby soon and I couldn't stand the irony of the situation. I worked hard to focus my attention on her words and caught the tail end of what she was saying, ". . . abortion clinic. I can make you an appointment. Hopefully they will work you in tomorrow so you can get this taken care of."

I have no memory of the moments between her leaving the room and reentering it. I do, however, remember her next comment. "They can see you first thing tomorrow morning." I looked at her, with tears streaming down my face. *I was going to have an abortion. That's what she was telling me, right?* "You must hate me. You're so pregnant. You must hate having to schedule an abortion for me," I cried. She looked at me with compassion and said, "I would do the same thing if I were only sixteen."

She gave my mom the necessary paperwork and told me that I would need to get IV fluids to help with the severe dehydration I was experiencing. She asked me if I wanted to get the IV there, at her office, or if I wanted to go to the hospital. I quickly replied, "Hospital." I couldn't sit in that exam room for one more minute.

I don't recall leaving the doctor's office, riding in my mom's car to the hospital, walking into the hospital, being placed in a room, or anything else about the process. My next memory is laying in the bed, calling Bryan from the white corded phone laying on the table beside the bed. I don't remember the exact words we shared but I remember desperately wanting him to visit me while I lay there. We had been dating for almost three years. Sure, we had broken up a few times, but we had been such a big part of each other's lives for years. Not only was he part of this nightmare, he was my best friend. I wanted him to comfort me and talk to me and help me through this. I wanted him to acknowledge his part in this situation. He couldn't come, though. He already had plans with someone he would be attending college with in the fall. They had planned it days ago. According to him, he didn't have feelings for her, but he believed it would be wrong to cancel the plans last minute. Afterall, he was meeting people that would be living in his dorm. He just wanted to know some folks when he started school in a couple of months.

My heart was broken. I couldn't wrap my mind around what was happening within my body and on top of that, I felt as if I wasn't even important enough for my boyfriend of three years to visit me in the hospital. Not to mention, I wouldn't be in this predicament if not for him. I was less important than a girl he had never even met in person. Right then and there, my value plummeted, in my own eyes at least.

As I hung up the phone, the nurse entered and started my IV. She hung two bags on the stand and attached them to the tubes. "These are just meds to help with hydration and nausea. You'll be feeling sleepy soon, try to get some rest." She walked toward the door, turned off the light, and exited the room.

I now laid by myself in the cold, dark room. My mind was dominated by fear, rejection, worry, and anxiety. Bryan's decision to go see another girl instead of me, on the day I needed him most, had shredded my heart into a thousand tiny pieces. I was utterly alone, not just in this room, but with this terrible problem. Tears spilled down my cheeks and streamed onto my pillow. As the medication took effect, I drifted off to sleep.

I thought it was all a dream when I first awoke from the haze. Now I realized, it was more real than anything I had ever experienced before.

2

My Childhood

WE WERE A LOVELY little family of four. A beautiful mother, a successful father, and two kids just living out the "American Dream." I was a daddy's girl, no doubt about it. I remember always wanting my daddy to have the best piece of pie or the largest cookie because I considered him the "King" of our home. Those specific words played over and over in my young mind. "Daddy is the king and I am

My family in 1985

his little princess." I believed he hung the moon, and something tells me, he believed the same about me.

Around age five I became aware of something disturbing the peaceful life we lived out. No one would have ever guessed anything was less than wonderful within our home. Our family looked picture perfect. In fact, my dad was the best, most respected photographer in our town and our family pictures were seen by everyone that visited his studio or read the town's newspaper.

There was a great deal of fear and anger present in our home. My young mind was filled with thoughts that no five-year-old should ever have to think about. I saw things I should have never seen. I lived in fear of my dad's anger.

Over the next few years things worsened but were still hidden. Most people continued to see the flawless family we pretended to be. A few neighbors and family members noticed that things weren't always as they seemed. Our babysitters were probably the most aware. I remember one sweet teenage girl getting caught in the middle of an argument. She left my brother and me eating macaroni and cheese at our kitchen table because she couldn't handle the atmosphere once my parents arrived home. This was the atmosphere we lived in constantly.

I don't know what happened to cause this rift in our family. As I look back now, I can see Satan having a hay-day in our lives. When we give into darkness, even just a little bit, it will seep in and mess up every possible area of our lives it can. Our enemy is tricky, sneaky, and always out to get us.

It's no secret that during this time my father had an on-going affair with an employee at his photography studio. The relationship went on and on and eventually they conceived a child, my half-sister. While my memories don't provide a detailed timeline, I believe this was the event that resulted in the decision for divorce. As horrible as it is for a man to have an affair and an illegitimate child while still married, that was only half of the horror we lived. My mom endured a lot. She has never received the honor and acknowledgement she deserves because of the secrecy of our situation. I will probably never know all that she dealt with, but I do know she kept going for my brother and me. She has often said that Philippians 4:13 carried her through that time. "I can do all things through Christ who gives me strength." He did give her strength and helped her carry on through what would be a nightmare for most.

At age nine my parent's divorce became official. We lived through four years of hell, but we made it. When I look back over those years most of my memories are ones I wish I had never experienced. Somehow my memory seemed to capture all the bad days, even though I feel certain there were many good ones as well. One of the most difficult things for me during this time was the sorrow I felt for my father. I was the epitome of a daddy's girl, even though I knew his flaws. I saw him in a way other people didn't. I knew the wrong choices he made, and I lived through the turmoil those choices caused, but I still loved him to pieces. I saw a broken man who needed to be loved and I chose to be the one who loved him. It's easy to look at our situation and see my dad as the bad guy. Looking back, I know God gave me the ability to see my father as a victim of Satan's schemes even though, at the time, I knew nothing about such things. My dad did terrible things, but his life was turned upside down as well. It seemed no part of his existence was untouched by darkness. It must have been such a difficult time for him. My heart aches for him, even now, because that couldn't have been the life he dreamed of having for himself or his family.

When my parents' divorce was final, I began spending every other weekend with my dad. For a while I slept on the floor of his room at my grandmother's house. I remember the sound of the wind rushing through the window at night as I laid there on a little blow up mattress. I remember eating my Grandma Doris' biscuits and gravy, listening to her play the organ, and playing with her three-legged cat. It was an odd time, but also held some sweet memories. In time, he moved into a little white house on Pickerd Circle . . . the "Pickerd Circle house" as we called it. My dad let me pick out the bunk bed for my room, one that I would be sharing from time to time with my half-sister. I also helped decorate the rest of the house and had so much fun picking out carpet colors and furniture. We went grocery shopping and cooked meals together. We had several cats, one of which had babies that were the most adorable little creatures I had ever laid eyes on. Things weren't perfect in that house but there was some normalcy and a lot of happiness there. I only saw my dad on Wednesdays and every other weekend but when we were together, it was like old times. I wasn't afraid and there seemed to be no anger most of the time.

I was getting used to this new way of life, half of the time with my dad, half of the time with mom. Little did I know; some other pivotal things were about to happen. A few months after the divorce was final, my mom met what probably seemed like a Knight in Shining Armor to her. To me as well, in many ways. The day I met him, I loved him immediately and I asked, "Will you please marry my mom?" I saw a happiness in her that I had not seen in a long time and I didn't want it to fade.

One afternoon, I was doing my homework at the childcare center when the director (the same one who employed me years later) came to my classroom and took me to her office. I entered the room and saw my mom sitting there, beaming. She had some news for me. She and her knight had eloped.

For the first time in years I felt peace. My mom was happily remarried and loved. My dad was rebuilding his life at the Pickerd Circle house and I enjoyed spending time with him there. Everyone was safe. Everything was okay.

For a moment.

Until the day my dad disappeared. He left town. Just vanished. My ten-year-old mind could not make sense of it. *Where had he gone? Why did he leave me? When would he be back? Would I ever see him again? What did I do wrong?*

No reason had been given. No goodbye. Nothing.

The heartbreak that followed cannot be adequately described with words. My dad was my world and always had been. I had loved him even when there were a hundred reasons not to. I had believed the best about him when no one else did. I had looked forward to every weekend I spent with him and enjoyed everything we did together. I had endured years of darkness and still called out the light in him.

And now he was gone. Not because of illness or death. Not because of a job forcing him to change locations. He was gone because he chose to leave.

As an I adult, I believe there is much more to the story, though I still don't know the reason he left. I can only imagine the heartbreak he must have suffered. I believe his hell continued even though I thought life was good again. Our times together were probably bits of joy and solitude for him while the rest of his days were still bitter and dark. Without me knowing it, he must have had more than he could handle. The enemy had seeped in years prior and wreaked havoc on his life. Hopelessness settled in on his heart and he fled.

I cried myself to sleep night after night. I dreamed of seeing him again but began to believe I never would. The ache in my heart was too much. I subconsciously started pushing all feelings away. It felt easier than dealing with the emotions. Sadly, this would become my way of dealing with everything, for many years to come.

3

With My Daddy Gone

MY DAD'S PRESENCE HAD always been a vital part of my life, even during the darkest times. Others probably couldn't understand it, but I needed him in my life regardless of the turmoil his choices had caused. His absence altered me. As an impressionable pre-teen, his departure acted like a line drawn in the sand. Fear of rejection took up residence in my heart almost immediately. I would never be the same.

The days turned into weeks. The weeks turned into months. I was growing up without the most important man in the world to me. My mom's Knight in Shining Armor never once tried to take the place of my father but he stood in the gap when my dad wasn't there. He never allowed anyone to speak ill of my dad and he always reassured me that one day I would see him again.

Life just goes on, although it feels like it shouldn't. Over time I became very good at pushing my feelings away and ignoring the crucial issues in my life. I thought of my dad less and less because it was easier that way. My brother was adopted by our stepdad and changed his last name. That option was available to me as well, but I just couldn't do that to my dad. I tried my best not to think of him but my love for Daddy remained.

One year, at Christmastime, my uncle drove up our driveway with a gift for me and one for my brother. He wouldn't enter our house with the gifts, I'm not sure why, so we stood in the storage building behind our home to open the gifts. I slowly opened the gift, noticing the handwriting that I knew so well. *This really was from my dad. He hadn't forgotten me.* Inside the box was a beautiful silver chain with an elegant cross pendant. It was gorgeous and I loved it immediately, although the only meaning it held for me at that time was my dad. I continuously pondered how his hands had held the necklace and wrapped the gift. *Maybe he did still love me.*

Along with all the changes of entering middle school, came new friends and more distractions. I found myself desperately seeking approval from anyone who would dish it out. Mostly, that approval came from bad influences. At twelve years old I was smoking cigarettes, drinking alcohol, and smoking weed with several older kids. I found all my value in whether others liked me or not, and I would do whatever they were doing, just to feel accepted and invited. Anything to avoid rejection.

In April of 1996 my father was located by our county's child support department. I don't know where they found him or where he had been, but I remember being dumbfounded by the news.

My mom and stepdad offered to take me to see him. I hadn't seen him in so long. Even though I probably looked mostly the same, I was a completely different person. I was terrified to see him, but I couldn't choose to hurt him the way he had hurt me.

I sheepishly walked into my grandmother's house looking for him. I heard his voice from a distance and the daddy's girl inside of me leapt with joy. He really was back! I found him in the room where I once slept on the floor every other weekend. The window was open, and the wind was rushing through it again. So many memories. So much time had passed. So much sadness. But there he was. I could touch him. I could talk to him.

My memory of the conversation is vague and faded. I don't know what we discussed or what words were shared but I remember well the heartbreak of seeing him, so broken and so tired. I couldn't shake the feeling that he had been caught. He didn't really want to be here. He had to be now. I left feeling emotionally exhausted and a bit angry. For years I had loved him when no one else did. When he left, I remained loyal to him and loved him whole-heartedly even though I pushed thoughts of him away, a form of self-protection, I suppose. And now, I was expected to feel sorry for him? Now, I was supposed to pretend like he chose to come back and be happy to see him? My emotions were wild. I couldn't figure out how to navigate such a sticky yet slippery situation. So, I avoided it, something I had gotten very good at doing.

I wish I could say that things were quickly mended but honestly, I don't recall seeing my dad for a while after that. In fact, I don't remember when I saw him again or when I thought about him again. I had grown accustomed to pushing away things that caused pain within me. So, that's exactly what I did.

A few months later, on June 28, 1996, a friend was spending the night at my house. Out of boredom we decided to visit someone that lived down the street from me. I didn't know any of the kids in my neighborhood. I had lived there my whole life, but my childhood had been riddled with things that took my attention from normal "kid things." I never played with any neighbors except the ones right across the street. I had never gone past their house on my bike. I had never explored like most kids do.

My sleepover buddy went to school with several kids in my neighborhood and knew exactly where they lived. So, she led the way. First, I was introduced to Lydia. The most adorable blonde girl with such a sweet spirit. From the moment I met her I knew I wanted to be her friend. She had kind eyes and obviously wasn't hurting inside, the way I was. I'm not sure why, but the three of us decided to walk down the road to see if another kid was home. We strolled down the street, talking and giggling. As we came near the house, we didn't see anyone riding bikes or playing basketball. So, we walked up the hill to the side of the house. As we inched our way up the driveway, my eyes spotted a blonde, shirtless, teenage boy lifting weights. Seriously, could he have been any more appealing to a thirteen-year-old girl?

I was immediately smitten. Bryan Shaw was fifteen years old and incredibly cute. I couldn't believe he had lived right here, on my street, my entire life and I had never seen him. My mind went wild with ideas of getting to know him and being able to spend time together since we lived on the same street.

Some other neighborhood kids joined us, and we all ended up spending the day together talking, walking around, playing duck-duck-goose in the "triangle," which was a common area in the neighborhood. I spent the entire day hoping Bryan liked me as much as I liked him. At the end of the night, my friend and I said goodbye to Bryan at the bottom of his driveway. Right there, under the streetlights, I remember thinking, "I'm going to marry that boy one day!"

That same night, as soon as I walked through my front door, I pulled out the piece of notebook paper with Lydia's name and phone number on it. I didn't know her, but I called her anyway. I had to get the inside scoop on this blonde-haired neighbor. Lydia and I talked for a while. This conversation would be the beginning of a friendship that would carry me through my high-school years.

4

The Boy That Changed My Life

As soon as I woke up the following morning, I started thinking about Bryan! I wondered if he had also been thinking of me. I wanted to see him again just to see what might happen. I was a ball of nerves, but Lydia and I spent the day, once again, with Bryan and other neighborhood kids. This was literally so much fun for me. I had never spent hours with neighbors just talking and exploring and laughing. My childhood had been consumed with other things. It was so refreshing for me. Not to mention, the time I got to spend with Bryan was beyond exciting. I liked everything about him. He was funny and confident and probably the cutest boy I had ever laid eyes on.

Throughout that second day together it became very clear, Bryan liked me too. We flirted and laughed and wanted to be next to each other as we all strolled through the neighborhood. After spending hours together, the sun faded away and we said goodbye once again, in front of Bryan's driveway. This time though, he kissed me!

After practically dancing all the way home, I skipped up to my room and plopped onto my bed. *He liked me! He really liked me!* I could barely wrap my mind around the idea that someone actually liked *me*.

The months that followed were exciting and fun. Bryan and I spent every minute we could together. Most of our days were spent at the "triangle" with our neighborhood friends or playing pool at Bryan's house. Our evenings were spent watching movies and hanging out at each other's houses.

When I wasn't with Bryan that summer, I fought against the life I had been living before meeting him. I had been spiraling so far downward. I had spent a lot of time with those older kids, doing things that even they shouldn't have been doing. Those "friends" still expected me to hang out with them and I was still so fearful of rejection. It was as if I was living two lives. Part of the time with Bryan, being a typical young teenager, head over hills for a boy in her neighborhood. The other part of the time in the awkward, inappropriate, unhealthy lifestyle I had created for myself. I felt torn between the two and desperately wanted to please everyone.

In time, Bryan found out about the other lifestyle I was leading. He begged me to quit smoking and didn't understand why I would even want to be involved with those "friends." He had never felt completely lost which led to seeking out acceptance anywhere he could get it. There was no way he could understand. Many arguments and hurt feelings resulted.

Even though things were a little crazy, Bryan began inviting me to youth group on Wednesday nights. At first, I only went because he invited me, but in time, I started to really enjoy it. I had grown up going to church with my family. We went on Sunday mornings but other than memorizing the books of the Bible, I didn't learn much. I don't recall truly learning anything about Jesus or ever being told that I could have a personal relationship with Him. I always viewed God as a very distant, hateful Deity. I figured He must have forgotten about me or never cared about me to begin with. Honestly, I barely thought of God at all because I had never witnessed someone living their life for Him or been taught how to talk to him or been told that I mattered to him.

Those first few weeks of youth group were like water to a parched land for me. Pastor Pete shared so many things that I desperately needed to hear. I made new friends and became aware of a way of living that had never occurred to me previously. These people lived a righteous life. They didn't drink or smoke or lie or cheat. They didn't abuse one another with their words or fists. They didn't use foul language or bash one another behind their backs. They were evidence to me that there was more. *Maybe God wanted more for me?*

As the summer came to an end, I dreaded the upcoming year, my freshman year in high school. Although Bryan and I lived on the same street, I went to a county school while he and the other neighborhood friends went to a city school. Middle school had been such a weird time for me. I had a few friends but no close relationships. There wasn't really anyone I looked forward to seeing or anything about the school I wanted to be a part of.

As the school year began, I knew quickly that I didn't belong there. It wasn't the place I needed to be. There were still so many bad influences. I wished every school day away so that I could be back in my little neighborhood with the new friends I had made, especially Bryan. I did well in my classes but had no real motivation or desire to succeed in this school. It just wasn't the right place for me.

Sept. 21, 1996

Our First Picture Together

In September of 1996, Bryan invited me to a Billy Graham Crusade with the youth group. I honestly had no idea what a crusade was, but I was eager to go. That night I heard songs and words that I had never heard before. I couldn't tell you even one of those songs or words now, but I can say with certainty that God used each one to minister to my heart and lead me to Himself. Near the end of the evening, Billy Graham invited those who wanted to surrender their lives to Jesus to come down to the football field. I leaned over to Bryan and whispered, "I want to go, will you go with me?" We walked together, step after step, and he held my hand as I gave my life to Jesus.

That night forever changed my life.

5

A New Beginning

IT WOULD BE AN easy move. It was the school I was assigned to go to anyway. I would have a fresh start with new friends and less negative influences. And, most importantly, I wouldn't dread every school day.

I had all my reasons lined out, ready to talk to my mom. Much to my despair, she didn't even want to hear my arguments. She said no and that was final.

As the fall days grew shorter and the end of the semester was inching closer, I became desperate. Since my mom wouldn't agree to my idea, I decided to talk to my dad, even though my relationship with him was lacking. I explained all the reasons switching schools would be best, and he seemed to agree with me. But he didn't think my mom would want to hear his input.

My stepdad always encouraged a relationship between me, my mom, and my dad. So, I decided to talk with him about all of this. *Maybe he could talk some sense into her?* I honestly have no idea what conversations were had or what finally changed my mom's mind, but before the semester ended, she agreed to let me begin the spring semester of my freshman year at a new school. I'll give credit to all of my dads, especially the Heavenly One, who I had recently discovered and so desperately needed to experience.

As the weeks approached, I could barely contain my excitement. I would be attending a new school with my new neighborhood friends. It seemed like a dream. I couldn't wait!

The new school year began, and a fresh start unfolded. It was scary being the new kid. It was hard, in fact. But from the very beginning, it was clear this was a wonderful choice for me. I quickly began making friends, joining extracurricular activities, and embracing the new life God had given me. A few weeks into the first semester, I was tested for academic giftedness and scored very high. I spent years at my previous school without anyone noticing I was a gifted student. It only took this new school a handful of weeks to see that I wasn't in the classes I needed to be in. Finding out that information and being switched to more advanced classes was a confidence booster and a game-changer! I suddenly found a desire to do my very best and succeed with every task, assignment, and test.

Switching schools truly was like a brand-new start for me. I was becoming a completely different person. I barely recognized myself but at the same time, I knew that this was who I really was. I was confident I was traveling down the path the Lord had destined for me.

While I wish I could say that Bryan and I lived out the perfect high school sweetheart fairy tale, that wouldn't be true. We had a lot of ups and downs. A lot of our problems were probably rooted in my dishonesty the first few months of our relationship. I had been living two lives. There were times I had been deceptive. I was so desperate not to lose the one person who wanted me, so I hid things that I thought might cause him to flee from me. It was self-preservation but it only caused more problems. Even though I had left that other life behind, the problems remained. Bryan and I broke up many times. There were times we treated each other unfairly and times we showed each other tremendous grace.

As God began to transform me and create a new heart within me, I was torn again. My life was so much better. I had so many reasons to be incredibly grateful. My whole world had changed, and I was actually enjoying my life, most days. But behind all of that changing and living, was still a broken little girl who desperately desired acceptance and love. My life looked completely different, but I had not worked through any of the rejection and pain. At this point, I probably looked like a very healthy, happy teenager. On the surface things were good. Below the surface, however, was a different story.

Since I had barely shared the heartache over my childhood with anyone and had learned to suppress and conceal the pain, no one really noticed how rejected I felt. Because of this, I sought love and acceptance from Bryan. Girlfriend/boyfriend relationships should involve love and acceptance to some degree, but a fifteen-year-old girl shouldn't be finding the love she needs and the acceptance she desires from anyone other than God. Doing so will almost always lead her astray.

Even though Bryan and I broke up from time to time, like most young couples do, we never stayed apart long. Our relationship wasn't healthy, but we did love each other! Most of our days consisted of school, extracurricular activities, homework, and spending time together. I learned over time how to get his attention and how to feel desired and loved by him. He was a teenage boy with raging hormones, and I was a teenage girl who wanted nothing more than to be desired. That combination leads to a lot of moments alone together, enjoying too much of each other.

All the while, we were steady attenders of youth group, and Sunday morning worship. We sang together in the worship band and participated in the church skits and plays. We had even been baptized on the same evening. I read my Bible daily and journaled my prayers. The only thing that didn't seem to line up was the depth of my relationship with Bryan. I prayed for forgiveness and knew that sex before marriage was wrong. It's funny though, it never seemed possible to stop doing it. I knew what teenage boys wanted (or at least I thought I did) and my fear of rejection was like a giant I couldn't face. I was terrified of losing the one person who wanted me. I would have done almost anything to avoid being rejected again.

6

Getting His Attention

THROUGH THE UPS AND downs of our relationship, Bryan and I always dreamed of a future together. I remember sitting in "the triangle" under a little tree, talking about the family we would have one day. We counted down the years until we could get married and wished away the time. We would talk about what our children might look like and what their names would be.

My Sweet Sixteen with Bryan and my dog, Mozart

Bryan's first car was a hand-me-down from his parents. Even though he didn't like it one bit, at sixteen years old, he drove a little white station wagon. My stepdad always called us "the little married couple" because we would go everywhere together in that station wagon.

As we grew older together, I continued to find my security in Bryan, and any time that security felt threatened, I would do all that I could to try and make him want me more. What I ate and what I wore, how much I exercised and even what I was willing to do, all hinged on whether or not I felt wanted and loved by him. That's a lot to put on the shoulders of a teenage boy! It was only a matter of time until that heavy burden would be unappealing to him, and now I can fully understand why.

When 1999 rolled around, things were beginning to change in our lives. Bryan would be graduating in June and heading off to college in August. He was excited and I was scared to death. In early spring, Bryan decided it was time to get to know a few more of those "fish in the sea." He broke up with me and began dating another girl. After a few weeks he dropped that girl and found a new one. It's typical teenage boy stuff, I would imagine, but to me, it was devastating. I was an absolute mess but tried to carry on. Somehow, I was able to keep up my grades and extracurricular activities. After a couple of weeks, Bryan began calling me again and we began seeing each other from time to time. As a senior, he had a free lunch period and since I was a part of the school newspaper, I could leave school during that same time. Many days I found myself at Bryan's house during his lunch break. I would often bring him lunch but mostly, I went just for the chance to be with him and hopefully, cause him to want me again. Day after day, I would go to his house, just hoping that he would decide I was the one he really wanted.

Make no mistake about it, I knew exactly what I was doing. I never created a game plan or thought it out step by step, but I knew how to get his attention and that's exactly what I did. Mostly, I just wanted him to desire me but looking back now, I know my heart was utterly broken and I believed this was the only way he would love me again.

As prom approached, I kept waiting on him to ask me. It slowly became clear to me that my attempts to regain his affection weren't quite good enough. My fears were confirmed when he asked another girl to prom. She attended a different school and he seemed smitten with her. For some reason, though, he still spent many of his afternoons with me. I kept hoping maybe he would change his mind and invite me to prom instead, but he didn't. I finally began to accept it as fact . . . he didn't want me. Even though he sure did act like it during those lunch breaks.

I had to face it. I wouldn't be going to prom with Bryan. My heart ached every time the thought crossed my mind. While I wanted to hide under a rock, I knew I couldn't do that. So, I asked some friends to help me find a prom date and they gladly suggested someone to ask. He was a sweet guy, a year younger than me, and he wasn't friends with Bryan. I worked up the nerve to ask him. At this point, I felt so utterly undesirable, I seriously doubted he would agree to go with me. But, much to my surprise, he said yes!

In the weeks leading up to prom, I stopped spending my lunch breaks with Bryan. I tried to focus on the friendships that meant so much to me and tried to get to know my soon-to-be prom date. Even though this new boy liked me, I didn't believe I was worthy of anyone's attention since I was unwanted by the boy I loved so much.

On prom day, my friends and I got ready together, my date and I took all the obligatory photos, and then a huge group of us went out for dinner. I was having fun and enjoying myself until the moment I saw him. He was so handsome and full of confidence. The only problem was, he had another girl on his arm. I didn't know whether to run away and cry or try to make him jealous. I chose the latter. I tried to have fun. My date and I danced. My friends and I laughed. All the while, I watched Bryan out of the corner of my eye. I wondered if he even noticed I was in the same room. I assumed he probably didn't

Captured prior to Prom 1999, I was blissfully unaware of my pregnancy

After prom, I attempted to move on. I went on a couple of dates and spent lots of time with friends. It was hard to imagine my life without Bryan since we had spent the last three years together, but I did the best I could. Just as I was making a little progress, Bryan broke up with his prom date and wanted me back. In some ways, this was the best news ever. In other ways, it was very hard for me.

There was no question though, I wanted to be with him. So, I joyfully ran right back into his arms. I felt the need to hide my relationship with Bryan from my friends because they didn't want me to get back together with him. Of course, that didn't work at all. So, my friends ended up being frustrated with me. I felt so torn. I was desperately trying to juggle all my emotions. *Why would he want me now? Was it only because things ended with the other girl? Had he missed me or just our lunch breaks together? Would he just dump me again?*

Things quickly went back to "normal" for us. We were spending a lot of time together and enjoying our last few weeks of school. Bryan was excited about college and began connecting with others that would be living in the same dorm. I tried not to show it, but I was terribly worried. I couldn't help but wonder what might happen to our relationship when he left for school. He said nothing would change and he would always love me, but I doubted that profusely. It was clear my concerns were not something he shared, and he never wanted to talk about it.

Soon, it was time for Bryan's high school graduation. I had a front row seat as he walked across the stage. I was so proud of him and so grateful to be a part of this huge event in his life.

He went to the beach with his friends for senior week and I started my summer job in the two-year-old class at the childcare center. When he got back from his trip, we spent the day together. We had lunch together. We could have never imagined how different life would be following that lunch date.

7

Discharged

A YOUNG NURSE ENTERED my hospital room, opened the blinds, and checked my IV. It was early. It couldn't have even been seven o'clock in the morning yet. She noticed my eyes were opened and said, "Good Morning, sweetheart." It quickly occurred to me that this nurse probably didn't know the full details of my situation. She told me my mom would arrive soon to take me home. She helped me go to the bathroom and took out my IV. She handed me a brush so I could fix my ponytail and then removed the ugly, brown, non-slip socks from my feet. She commented on my toenails. They were sky blue with white and yellow flowers painted on them. One of my friends had carefully painted the little flowers on just a few days before at a sleepover. *Oh, how simple life was then.*

The nurse couldn't get over the little flowers and even called another nurse into the room to look at them. About that time my mom entered the room and the remainder of the discharging process was completed. I walked out of the hospital door, still nauseous and quite groggy. My mom and I got into her car and drove home. It was still very early. The clinic wasn't open yet.

Once home and in my room, I laid in my bed and dialed Bryan's phone number on my neon corded phone. It rang several times. He answered. I have completely blocked out most of the words we exchanged during that conversation, but I do recall asking him to hold on while I rushed to the toilet to be sick again. I remember hearing my mom yell from downstairs that it was time for us to leave. With tears streaming down my face, I said goodbye and hung up the receiver.

Discharged

It was time to go.

We drove silently for about thirty minutes before arriving at the clinic. It was a small brick building. It didn't look like any doctor's office I had ever visited before, but it wasn't too ominous either. I remember walking in, signing my name on a clipboard, and then sitting in the waiting room. The room had several people in it. Most were reading magazines or books they had brought along. One lady was sleeping with her head propped up against the wall. My mom paid the fee and then sat down beside me. If we spoke, I don't remember what we said. In fact, I don't think anyone spoke. The room was heavy and dark. The feeling of depravity was almost tangible, but everyone did their best to ignore it.

"Tori," a middle-aged woman said, from an opened doorway nearby. *They're calling me.* I stood up and slowly walked toward the lady. I looked back at my mom and then went through the door. I heard it shut behind me and fear settled in.

I was led into a small room and given a cup for a urine specimen. The employee pointed toward the bathroom door and I followed the silent instruction. After filling the cup and handing it over, I was instructed to sit down while we waited on the pregnancy test results. It was the longest three minutes ever. The test was positive. Even though I already knew I was pregnant, seeing the test with a positive result shook me. *How did I get here? How could I have been so stupid? I never thought I would end up in a place like this.* Suddenly, I felt sick again. My nausea must have been noticeable because the nurse handed me a small trash can and encouraged me to carry it with me.

Since the test was positive, I could move on to the next phase of the process. I was asked numerous questions and placed into a room with at least ten other patients. Some were in their late twenties, some were college-aged, and some were young, but I looked the youngest, by far. I sat on a plush green padded chair, holding the trash can in case I got sick again. I took in the scene around me. Some of the ladies were staring off into the distance. A few others were watching a silent TV that flickered in the corner. There were also a couple of older girls giggling. *What in the world could be funny? Didn't they know where we were?* There were also a couple of employees sitting at a desk nearby. They were whispering about something (probably one of the patients) and rolling their eyes. One of them laughed belligerently and then stood up while calling out a patient's name. A twenty-something girl looked around the room and then followed the corridor to an exam room. My mind raced. *What was going to happen with her now? What waited on her in that room? Would she be ok?*

The concern must have been evident on my face. An older woman sitting beside me spoke up softly and said something like, "It's ok, darling. This is my third abortion. No one likes being here but it's better than the alternative." I let her words roll around in my head. Tears started pouring from my eyes. *Was it better than the alternative? Really?*

A few moments later another girl, probably about nineteen years old, looked at me and said, "I understand how you feel. This is *not* how I wanted to spend my Saturday." She was noticeably pregnant and seemed kind, but I don't think she really related to how I was feeling. In fact, I'm not sure I even knew what I was feeling. My eyes searched the room for some information about what would happen during the procedure. The walls had informative posters about women's health tacked on them, but abortion wasn't mentioned anywhere. I had no idea what to expect and no one offered to inform me.

I asked another lady, sitting nearby, if she knew whether it hurt or not. She had a gentle face and caring eyes. She turned toward me and said, "Yes, honey, it does." I asked her if she had done this before and she nodded yes. She didn't seem like someone that would have an abortion. But then again, neither did I. As not to scare me, she spoke vaguely for a few minutes about her previous experience. She commented on my trash can and chuckled. "Well, at least you shouldn't need that much longer," she laughed. It was an awkward attempt to lighten the mood. She was the only one who treated me like the terrified sixteen-year-old I was.

Another patient was called by a nurse from down the hall. It seemed like an eternity since the last patient had been summoned. A woman in her twenties quickly walked into an exam room. It was obvious she was ready to get this over with. A teenage girl, close to my age, entered the waiting room and sat down across from me. I watched her as she took in the surroundings. This was her first time too, I could tell. We didn't speak. Maybe we both knew talking would only lead to more tears.

The friendly woman who had shared her experience with me was called next. She winked at me as she left the waiting area. I knew it would soon be my turn. Only a couple of women who had been in the waiting room prior to me, remained. I watched the TV even though the sound was turned all the way down. Anything to distract my mind. The tears started flowing again. This time I didn't even realize it. My heart was just so overwhelmed with fear and disappointment. I felt so alone and rejected. I was so ashamed. A young woman who had recently entered the waiting area handed me a box of tissues. "It will be over soon," she said.

I heard my name called after what felt like at least an hour, probably longer. *Oh no! Was it really my turn?* I stood up, holding my box of tissues and my trash can. I carried them both down the dreary corridor and into a clinic room.

8

The Termination

MY HEART WAS POUNDING. My palms were sweating. My body was shaking. I looked around the dim room. The overhead lights were turned off and only two floor lamps lit up the room. It seemed a little odd for a medical facility, but I guess it was somewhat calming. The patient exam table was near the corner of the room. It had large black stirrups at the end of it and a long sheet of white paper covering the mauve padding. Near the bed there were several rigid, metal, unidentifiable utensils lined up on a small rolling table. Up against the wall, to the left of the table, was a bulky computer with wands and a keyboard attached, most likely an outdated ultrasound machine. Standing at the end of the table was a bendable light with a large metal lamp shade. In the opposite corner of the room, there was a short beige box on wheels. On top of the rolling box there were, what appeared to be, two large jars sitting in compartments. The jars had flexible plastic tubing attached. A few buttons and dials were in a line beside the jars. It was an intimidating machine. Beside it was a multi-level metal cart with folded gowns, towels, gloves, and other assorted items stacked on it haphazardly. On the wall, near the exam table, was a poster with the picture of a cute little kitten hanging from a tree limb. The caption said, "Hang in there!"

The nurse asked me to take off my clothes and put on the gown she had laid on a chair near the window. She left the room and when she reentered, I had done as she had asked. She placed my clothes in a cubby right outside the door and my flip flops were placed beside the exam table. She gestured toward the table and told me to lay down. As she left the room she added, "The doctor will be here in just a few minutes."

While I laid on the table, waiting on the doctor, my eyes traced every little hole in the ceiling tiles. I noticed how bleak and drab the room felt. It was the middle of June but there was a chill in the air. The room was small and as I waited, it felt as if it might close in on me.

I heard the creaking of the door as it opened. An overweight, older white woman with grayish blond hair entered the room along with a young, brunette nurse. They were both wearing scrubs. The nurse wore burgundy and the doctor wore teal. She also wore a white coat. The nurse took her place beside me while the doctor plopped down on a rolling stool and used her feet to pull herself closer to the table. The nurse had a gentle demeanor. Her presence was quite comforting. She asked how I was doing and then helped me scoot down on the table and place my legs in the stirrups. The doctor, however, had the bedside manner of a rock. She seemed annoyed and rushed. The nurse grabbed a light blanket from the metal cart nearby and covered my torso and upper legs. She commented on how my body was shaking. She thought I was cold, and a blanket might help. I knew otherwise.

The doctor pushed some buttons on the bulky computer and then wrote a couple of things in my chart before handing it off to the nurse. One of the wands was removed from its holder and she grabbed a tube of jelly from a basket. She pulled the blanket down and my shoved my gown up without even saying a word. The jelly was cold as she squirted it on my skin. Using the wand, she pushed on my lower abdomen, forcefully moving the wand around until she was satisfied with what she saw on the computer screen. She rattled off some information to the nurse, who wrote it all down in the chart. I was in a daze. I could hear her words but couldn't make sense of them. *Was she telling the nurse how fast the heart was beating? How old the baby was?* I asked her to repeat what she had said but she refused. I asked if I could see the ultrasound and she said hastily, "That's not a good idea."

Once her preliminary work was done, she rolled her stool toward the big beige box and pulled it closer to the table. The nurse pushed a lever on the side of the table which caused the stirrups to rise higher, almost lifting my body completely off the bed. She slid a disposable towel beneath me and laid one on the floor below. *I thought I would be asleep for this part.* I looked over to the nurse with tears rolling down my cheeks and whispered, "I'm so scared." She grabbed my hand and rubbed it with hers. "It doesn't take too long," she offered quietly. I closed my eyes, wishing it were over.

I heard the doctor attaching the hoses to the utensils. The machine was being prepared and the doctor rolled it even closer. My body was shaking, and my heart raced. The doctor inserted a cold speculum and then using a long needle, she administered a local anesthetic. She stood and pushed on my tummy which caused me to squirm from the stinging pain. She allowed a few moments to pass so the anesthetic could take effect and then suddenly, I felt the procedure begin. The pain was sharp and strong. The pressure was intense. She used multiple tools and then tossed them onto the rolling cart close to the table. My body clenched and tightened. "Relax, you're just going to make it take longer," she exclaimed. I tried to force myself to be still, but the shaking was uncontrollable. After a few moments, the doctor turned on the machine. The sound of a vacuum filled the small room. The doctor moved the suctioning tool violently and turned off the machine. Then grabbing a second tube, she started suctioning again. It seemed as though the sound might never end. I could hear liquid rushing into the jar. The nurse told me not to hold my breath but to breathe and relax. That seemed impossible. Once the machine was turned off and the sound quieted, I could feel what can only be described as scrapping. The doctor looked up at me, as if joking with a friend, and said, "Don't want to miss anything."

When she pushed the machine back into the corner of the room, I was finally able to breath. The speculum was removed, and the doctor took off her gloves, tossing them on top of the tray of utensils. She left the room quickly. Probably moving on to another patient.

The nurse quietly assured me that everything was alright, and it was over. I laid on the table for a few minutes while the nurse completed my chart. She helped me sit up and warned me of the possible light-headedness. She was right. I felt like I might pass out. She laid a pair of mesh panties and a pad on the table beside me. She helped me put the items on and stand up. I glanced at the tray of medical supplies and tools. There was so much blood. The boxy machine was pushed back into the corner with a towel half-way covering it up. I got a glimpse of one of the partially filled jars. My stomach churned. The nurse held my hand, assisted me as I slipped into my flip flops, helped me sit in a wheelchair, and then wheeled me out into the recovery room. I carefully sat down in a black reclining chair. She pushed the chair back and encouraged me to rest a while. It wouldn't take long for me to fall asleep. I was utterly exhausted. Physically suffering and emotionally damaged. Part of me hoped I wouldn't wake up.

9

The Recovery

I awoke as another nurse helped someone sit in the chair beside me. I looked to my left and to my right. There were black reclining chairs lined up with clear, small tables next to each one. The room was covered in a dull pink and crème wallpaper. In a different setting it would have been a cheerful color. *What a joke.*

A heavy-set employee in burgundy scrubs brought over a soda with a few crackers. She laid them on the table beside me and went back to her desk. I took a couple of sips of the drink and nibbled on the cracker. The nausea overwhelmed me, and I laid back in the chair. A talk-show was playing on the television. I worked hard to focus my attention on it. Thoughts danced in and out of mind as I tried to figure out how this nightmare started. *I must have gotten pregnant during one of our lunch dates. I must have been pregnant at prom and didn't even know it. We weren't even dating and still I got pregnant because I thought I could make him want me. How could I have been so stupid?* I drifted in and out of sleep until the nurse in the burgundy scrubs brought over a little brown bag and placed it in my lap. I forced my eyes to open more and I looked in the bag. Inside I found six light-pink roundish discs. Pulling one out of the bag, I opened it and observed twenty-one little blue pills and seven little white pills. *It must be birth control.*

I shifted my weight in the chair and grimaced. *No one told me it would be this painful.* I looked around the room and saw several of the women I had spoken with earlier in the day. A few were sleeping, a couple were crying, and the others were looking down at the floor in a daze. All of us looked as if we had aged significantly in such a relatively short period of time. Even though we had spoken with one another in the waiting room, no one dared speak now. We all kept to ourselves, pretending we didn't know what we had just done. I remember wishing for the moments to pass so I could get out of this God-forsaken place and hide in my home.

Once my allotted recovery time had ended, the nurse got up from her desk, walked over to me, and asked how I was feeling. I didn't know how to respond. "I'm okay, I guess," I said. She grabbed my clothes from the cubby and helped me stand. She pointed toward the bathroom and instructed me to go in so I could get dressed. She stood at the door, watching me while I struggled to sit down on the toilet. I was right beside two other women that were also using the bathroom. I guess it shouldn't matter that there were no doors on the stalls. All of our dignity had been stripped from us, anyway, by this point. I was still light-headed and drained. It took all my energy to remove the dingy white gown and put my clothes back on. I stumbled out of the bathroom door. She pushed me in a wheelchair through the building, toward a different door than the one I entered. I surmised the staff didn't want the new patients to get a glimpse of the finished patients. If that happened, some might have reconsidered and left the clinic before going through with the abortion.

I don't recall the details but, my mom was there, ready to walk out with me. The nurse handed me instructions for care and my little brown paper bag. She looked at us with a grin and said, "Y'all have a good afternoon." Inwardly, I laughed dryly. *Was that even possible?* We turned and walked out the door into the warm air. The sun was blazing. The car was hot and so stuffy; it felt impossible to breathe. I shut the door and put on my seatbelt. It was over, or so I thought.

10

Back to Normal Life

DURING THE CAR RIDE home, I slept. All afternoon, all through the night, and into the next morning I continued to sleep. When I awoke, the nausea was gone but the pain re-mained. I forced myself to get out of bed, got dressed, and drove myself to church. My motive was not to seek for-giveness or be in God's pres-ence. It was more about silencing any rumors or gos-sip. I figured if I went to church that everyone would believe nothing had hap-pened, and everything was just fine. I had no reason to think anyone suspected a thing, but my mind had shift-ed, already, into self-protec-

Mountain Trip with Bryan's Family, July 1999

tion mode. Not even twenty-four hours after having an abortion, I was able to look and act as if it had never happened.

I only remember speaking of the abortion one time with Bryan, briefly and in a nonchalant manner. Life just went on. I went back to my summer job and spent a lot of time with Bryan, just soaking up those last weeks with him before he left for college. But the child I aborted entered my mind often, especially as I recovered physically from the procedure. I was able to quickly and easily push those thoughts away. I thought if I didn't acknowledge what I had done, maybe I could go on, like it had never happened.

I had another appointment at the clinic two weeks after the abortion for a follow up pregnancy test. It was just protocol, to make sure my body realized I was no longer pregnant. When I pulled up to the clinic, I sat outside for a while, just staring at the mismatched brick walls. I abhorred this place. I did not want to go back inside but I really didn't have a choice. I traced the outline of the bricks with my eyes, remembering what I had gone through inside those walls, just two weeks before. My heart raced and my stomach churned. I forced myself out of the car and walked inside. I hoped I could get this over with as quickly as possible!

Once inside, I was forced to walk the same path I had walked on my previous visit, except this time I entered alone. Signing in at the counter, sitting in the waiting room until my name was called, being ushered into a room and asked to give a urine sample. Each task scared me more and more. *Was I going through this all over again?* I remember sitting at the corner of a table in a small room waiting for the pregnancy test to be complete. The nurse looked at the test and then asked, "What are your plans this weekend?" My stomach dropped. "Why?" I asked. I was terrified. *Did this mean I was still pregnant, or something got left inside?* She could tell that her question had shaken me, hard. "Oh no, darling, I was just asking about your weekend. You don't have to come back again!" The calm that washed over me was incredible. I didn't have to go through it again. *Whew! Thank goodness!*

I finished answering the rest of the nurse's questions and made my way back through the clinic. This time, as I exited the building and got into my car, I felt a sense of relief. I drove away, a sixteen-year-old girl trying her best to pretend the past few weeks had never happened and holding onto hope that I would never be bothered by this horrifying experience again. I was ready to move on with the rest of my life. And that is exactly what I did.

Less than a month after the abortion. I went on a mission trip with my youth group. I traveled twenty-six hours to Ouagadougou, Burkina Faso, which is in Africa. We spent a couple of weeks there painting a school, teaching Vacation Bible School, getting to know the people in the community, and sharing the gospel. It was truly an amazing experience. It seems strange, but while touring the market one afternoon, I purchased an African baby dress for my future daughter to wear.

At one point we encountered a large group of women, sitting in a circle, holding babies. They would pass the babies around the circle, feeding different ones as needed. No one seemed to mind whose breast a baby fed from, they all took turns feeding and burping the babies and then passed them on to another woman. Many of these ladies had never seen white women. As a nomadic tribe, they rarely stayed in one place for long. They had been introduced to white men but never white women. I remember the moms forcing their babies upon my friends and me. They wanted their babies to be held by the white women because they believed we would bring good luck for their children. We also had the honor of being some of the first to lay eyes on the grandchild of the tribe's leader. This baby was just a couple of days old. We were asked to hold her and to take photos with her. Holding that baby had a significant impact on me. I began to realize that if I was going to hide the abortion, I couldn't put myself in situations where I would be reminded of what I had done and allow my heart to get broken so easily.

I'm pictured here with the tribal leader's two-day old granddaughter.

After returning from the African continent, only a few weeks of summer remained until Bryan left for college. I was so worried. *Why would he want me, the damaged high school girl, when he would most likely meet many perfect, beautiful college girls?* I went with his family as they helped him unpack and prepare his dorm room. I didn't want to leave. I wished with all my heart that I could stay there with him but, that wasn't possible. I remember the ride back home, without him. It felt like the longest car ride of my life. I knew things were changing, and I was torn up over it.

While he was home, I was able to continue pretending like the abortion had never happened. With him away at school, I was left to face reality or work incredibly hard to avoid it.

11

Senior Year

MY SENIOR YEAR OF high school began a couple of weeks after taking Bryan to college. It was a fun time. I had lots of great friends that I enjoyed spending time with, and an afterschool job at the childcare center. I took ballet every week and helped teach some of the littlest dancers in the company. I was also a part of our high school's choral ensemble, helped with our school newspaper, took courses at the community college nearby, was on the homecoming court, and took part in an internship at a local elementary school. I still went to church semi-regularly but wasn't involved any longer with the youth group. My life was busy. I was distracted almost all the time. I missed Bryan terribly and spent most of my down time worrying over what he was doing and who he was doing it with. Every couple of weeks I would spend the weekend with Bryan. I always told my mom I was staying with a friend who had graduated the same year as Bryan and was attending the same college. I never stayed with her once. I don't recall my mom ever questioning me so, I spent the night with Bryan, in his dorm room, as often as I could. I got very familiar with college life on the weekends. I made a lot of friends and had a lot of inappropriate fun. All the habits I had been able to rid myself of a couple of years before, came flooding back into my life. As soon as I witnessed Bryan partying and recklessly enjoying life, I considered that a green light for me to do the same. Those weekends were filled with alcohol and illicit drugs such as ecstasy, LSD, and mushrooms. We spent a great deal of time at a nearby fraternity house and I became an expert at chugging from a beer bong and doing keg stands. I was becoming a person I didn't even recognize.

Somehow, on the drive home each weekend, I would morph back into a very sweet high schooler. By all accounts, I was living, two completely different lives. I was an excellent student and did well with virtually everything in which I applied myself. I exercised daily and was careful about what I ate (mostly because in my mind, I could never be skinny enough). I had very good grades and enjoyed my internship in a kindergarten class immensely. I had a small role in the high school musical and enjoyed every minute of it. I earned a full academic scholarship and counted down the days until I could be away at college every day.

My senior prom, 2000

Unlike the year before, Bryan was my date for the senior prom. We had a wonderful time together but didn't stay long. After dinner and a few dances, we went back to Bryan's dorm and partied hard. I even brought some of my high school girlfriends along that time. A portion of my two worlds colliding was somewhat odd but it was bound to happen eventually.

The last several weeks of school were busy and exciting. My mind was occupied with all the things I had going on. I never took even a moment to think about what had happened almost a year before.

The only quiet moments I had, I spent worrying over what Bryan might be doing. I drowned out any feelings that popped up and worked hard to be pleasing to everyone. Still, deep down, my biggest concern always boiled down to being accepted and liked, especially by Bryan.

On June 2, 2000 I graduated with honors from high school. I had so much to be proud of, especially since I spent so much of my time that year drinking and popping pills. The following day, my friends and I left for the beach to celebrate "Senior Week." It was a wild and crazy week, but we all had a great time, mostly. Some of my friends, who hadn't spent a weekend at college with me, got a glimpse of the other side of me and it was a bit of a shock. Bryan and a few of his friends came to stay with me the last couple of days of the trip. I welcomed their familiar way of enjoying themselves, partying way too hard, and ended up pushing away some of my high school friends, regrettably.

That summer was hurried and busy. A couple of trips and a new part-time job, plus shopping and preparing for my dorm room, kept me busy and helped the summer go by quickly. The day I would move into my dorm could not arrive quick enough. I counted down the moments.

12

Dorm Life

I REMEMBER THE DAY I moved into the dorm so clearly. My mom, my step-dad, and my dad moved all my things in and helped me arrange my room. As they were about to leave, I remember hugging my dad tightly and sobbing. There was a sudden rush of emotion that I hadn't expected. My heart was still so broken and so fragile.

Over the next couple of days, I made some new friends in my dorm and was reacquainted with many of the friends I had made previously. Since I had spent so much time in this dorm with Bryan and had walked the path through the woods to the fraternity house many times, I was the leader of the pack for the big blowout party to kick-off the 2000–2001 year. Bryan later told me he couldn't believe his eyes, as he watched a huge group emerge from the wood line near the fraternity house. Tons of people led by little ol' me.

A seventeen-year-old honor graduate with a full college scholarship and a very bright future, was also one of the biggest partiers at the university during that time. A bit of an oxymoron.

A month or so into the academic year, a friend told me that Bryan had been cheating on me throughout his freshman year. All those nights I had spent worrying over what he was doing, had been for good reason. When I wasn't at college with him, he had been with numerous other girls. My fears were validated and suddenly my life was closing in around me. I was so broken, so tired, so hopeless, and so consumed with hatred toward myself. *Why was it so easy for the people I loved most to reject me? What was wrong with me?*

Bryan and I broke up and suddenly all my reasons for choosing to attend that specific college were invalid. I questioned everything. I was smothered by depression and wished every day away. I don't remember attending classes or being on campus. I felt like the biggest idiot and imagined all the "friends" I had made during Bryan's freshman year laughing behind my back every time I came to visit. I was absolutely heart broken and humiliated. I avoided those friends at all costs.

I decided it might be best to join a sorority. That way I could meet new friends and have a sisterhood of ladies to lean on. My roommate and I both participated in rush and both got bids from the same sorority. We moved together, to a different dorm which housed all the sororities. We were very busy learning all about sorority life, getting to know our sisters, and preparing to pledge. That's when I met Summer and Erica, who became very supportive friends. I spent most of my time self-medicating to relieve my pain and attempting to pretend like I was okay, again. I quit my current job and started as a hostess at a well-known restaurant. I cut all my hair off, a cute pixie cut. I worked

Freshman Year of College

out daily and went to the tanning bed a few times a week. I even got my tongue pierced. I thought, maybe if I changed my life, my appearance, and got in perfect shape, maybe then someone would consider me too valuable to abandon.

One night, while at a club near campus, my friends warned me that Bryan was there too. I remember the way he looked, just like it was yesterday. He was more handsome than ever. So cute that even my girlfriends pointed it out. The two of us had always been like magnets. If we were in the same room, we would be drawn to one another. And of course, we ended up talking and dancing. At the end of the night, Bryan asked me to go on a date the next day. I was torn. I knew most people wouldn't even consider the idea but, I wasn't most people, and this *was* the love of my life. Erica and Summer spent more time with me than anyone, at this point, which meant they had seen my heartache and how much I loved Bryan. They encouraged me to go on just one date. So, that's what I decided to do.

The following afternoon Bryan picked me up at my new dorm. We drove around for a while, had dinner, and went back to his apartment to talk. I had been to this apartment hundreds of times before, but it felt so foreign as I walked in. I hadn't told anyone else in my sorority that I would be spending time with Bryan because I knew they would try to talk me out of it. So, I was sneaking around to see the boy I loved because I was worried what some girls I barely knew might think. *Heaven forbid they be unhappy with me.* But then again, I didn't need to be abandoned or rejected by anyone else.

Bryan was kind and gentle and answered all my questions. He held me as I cried and tried his best to explain himself. He apologized profusely and said the past several weeks without me had been the worst weeks of his life. I welcomed each and every word but wondered if any of it were true. He wanted us to try dating again and of course, I wanted that more than anything too, but I was so scared and unsure. I was a wreck.

Continuing to hide everything from most of the people I interacted with daily, I started spending more time with Bryan. Summer and Erica became my absolute best buds because they listened to me and supported me. They were always there for me. They also came over to Bryan's apartment often, to hang out and party with us. I honestly don't know what I would have done without their friendships and sincere concern during that time.

One evening stands out in my memory above the rest. It was late. Everyone in the apartment was already asleep when we heard a loud, continuous bang at the door. The knocking persisted until someone answered it. Then suddenly the knocking started at Bryan's closed door. I heard the voice of a guy, whom I didn't recognize, saying he had come to get me. He explained that my sorority sisters were getting me out of this place, whether I liked it or not. There was also a lot of yelling by some girls who had barged into the house as well. I seriously wondered if it could be a dream. *Could this really be happening? I mean, I knew they wouldn't approve of me being with Bryan, but I never imagined they would act like this.* On the other side of the door I had folks yelling at me to get out of the apartment and come back to my dorm. On my side of the door, I had Bryan reminding me that I was an adult, could make my own choices, and didn't have to leave with them. The harsh words they screamed were hurtful and belittling and only made me want to stay inside the room more. They finally gave up and stopped banging and knocking when they realized I wasn't coming out. Sleep didn't come easy that night, but the tears sure did.

The next evening, even though I dreaded it immensely, I returned to my dorm room. There was an intervention, of sorts, waiting on me. I sat through the most ridiculous night of interrogation and berating. These girls had only known me for a couple of months. They didn't know all the circumstances behind our break-up. They had no idea what my life had involved until this point. They couldn't have known that the two of us had already conceived and aborted a child. They had no clue how long Bryan and I had been together or the dreams we had for our lives together. They just assumed they knew what was best for me and made it absurdly clear how they felt. During that meeting I discovered my "big sister" in the sorority had been one of the girls Bryan was involved with the previous year.

I can't begin to describe the embarrassment and betrayal I felt. *Why in the world had she chosen me as her "little sister" when she knew the truth all along?* During rush she had befriended me and encouraged me to pledge her sorority. During a few of my visits to see Bryan during his freshman year, we had all spent time together and honestly, I really liked her. All the while, I was just the clueless high school girl. *I was just a big joke.*

The next day, I asked an acquaintance, who lived in a dorm across campus, if I could move in with her. I knew her roommate wouldn't be returning the following semester and since it was almost Christmas break, it seemed perfect. Thankfully, she said yes. I avoided going in my dorm as much as possible and then, and as soon as the new room was ready, I quit the sorority and moved all my belongings over, one carload at a time.

13

God Carried Us

AFTER CHRISTMAS I CAME back to college ready for a fresh start. Somehow, I hadn't flunked my classes first semester even though I don't remember ever studying or doing assignments. I did get a C in one class, and that broke my heart. I had never even gotten a B in High School. I always earned straight A's. That C motivated me to focus more on my studies and try to put the horror of the first semester behind me.

I liked my new roommate but rarely stayed at the dorm. I might as well have been a "fourth" roommate at Bryan's apartment. The supposed friends that patronized me and tried to boss me around, caused me to run full force back into Bryan's arms. There were thousands of things left unsaid. We picked up our relationship right where we had left it before I found out that terrible news. All of this caused me to push my heartbreak down once again and pretend like everything was ok. I worked hard on my schoolwork but partied all the time as well. Erica and Summer were still my very best friends. They also spent a great deal of time at Bryan's apartment with us and his roommates. Between school, work, Bryan, my friends, and all the partying, my life was very full. The second semester of my freshman year was better than the first, but I still lived in a state of numbness and in fear of who would hurt me next.

Summertime came and went. I moved into an apartment near campus with two girls I had met in the last dorm I lived in. Things were great for a while but in time, the three of us no longer got along and I ended up moving back home with my parents. It was only a thirty-minute drive to and from school, so I finished out my sophomore year commuting from my parent's home.

As that academic year came to an end, neither Bryan nor I knew what our living arrangements would be for the following year. I had always dreamed that the first time we actually lived together would be right after we got married. Who was I kidding though? We basically lived together already. I battled with the decision in my heart but the summer after my sophomore year of college, Bryan and I moved into a big apartment in a gorgeous community about twenty minutes from campus.

My junior and senior year of college went smoothly. Bryan and I lived in our apartment together, I went to school in the mornings and worked in the afternoons. Bryan decided to work full time and had various jobs in those two years. On Valentine's Day of 2002, Bryan took me to my favorite restaurant, a Japanese Steakhouse. As the meal was coming to an end, he got down on one knee and asked me to marry him. I was shocked and so excited. I couldn't even get any words out. He looked at me and said, "Is that a yes?" I responded, "Yes!" Everyone at the hibachi style table clapped and cheered. The couple next to us even paid for our dinner. It was a magical night!

Over the next year and a half, we planned a wedding and prepared to spend the rest of our lives together! It was a fun time but also very busy for me. We decided it would be best to wait and have the wedding after I graduated with my teaching degree. So, my senior year of college I took classes, student taught in a kindergarten class, and worked at a daycare near our apartment. I graduated from college on May 14, 2004 and got married on June 5th.

Our Wedding

Our wedding day was perfect. We had a big wedding party of friends and a church full of guests. It was beautifully decorated, and everyone looked stunning. At five o'clock in the evening I walked down the aisle on my dad's arm. Halfway down the aisle, my dad offered my arm to my step-dad. My stepdad walked me the rest of the way. It meant so much to me, to have them both give me away, since they both meant so much to me. Seeing Bryan standing there, waiting on me, was truly a dream come true. This was a moment I had been waiting on for eight years. At twenty-one years old, I was marrying the love of my life. Thankfully, Bryan had tissues in his pocket because he knew I would cry, and I did! The emotion overwhelmed me. This was the best day ever!

After taking dozens of pictures, we hurried over to our reception. I was thrilled with the décor and our wedding cake. Seeing everyone there, clapping for us as we danced our first dance, is one of my favorite memories. We enjoyed a lovely dinner and danced the night away with friends and family. When we left in Bryan's little black car, it was covered in toilet paper and flour. We drove away, with cans clanking behind us, and spent our first night as a married couple in a lovely hotel. The next day we flew to Playa Del Carmen, Mexico for our honeymoon.

When I look back on that time, I see clearly that my graduation, our wedding, and the honeymoon had all been a gift from God. With all that our relationship had been through, there were many times that I wondered if marrying Bryan would ever be a reality. Honestly, I look back and wonder how we even made it through those college years. God carried us. Even though we made so many terrible choices and sinned against Him repeatedly, He carried us.

I will never forget returning home to our apartment. While unpacking our bags I saw a Bible laying on the bedside table. We were believers and even made Christ the center of our wedding day, but we never read the Bible. I was shocked to see it laying there. *Bryan must have been reading it the night before.*

Later that night he explained that he spent time reading and praying after our rehearsal dinner since he was alone in our apartment. He said he wanted to start our marriage off right and be the husband God called him to be. Those moments are etched in my memory. For the first time, I saw Bryan in a new way, as the leader of our family, desiring God to be the center of our marriage. I had never loved him more than I did right then.

14

First Years of Marriage

As we were getting adjusted to life as newlyweds, I was also searching for my first teaching job. I sent out multiple resumes and accepted the first kindergarten position I was offered. I spent the summer preparing my new classroom and enjoying time with my husband.

My first year of teaching was wonderful. I loved being a kindergarten teacher! There was a lot of paperwork and bickering among staff, which I had not witnessed while student teaching, but I enjoyed my students and had a whole lot of fun with them.

At the end of that school year, Bryan and I decided to buy our first home. I'm not sure why we even thought it was a good idea for us, since we were not financially stable. One of our friends had just become a licensed realtor and we were to be his first clients. After searching for a while to find something within our price range, we found a small, one-story home in a neighboring town. As we worked toward financing the house, it was becoming clear that buying a home might not work out. The numbers just weren't adding up in our favor. Even though it wasn't something I did often, I remember sitting at the bank, in a hard, blue chair, praying my heart out! Interestingly, the computer program the bank was using to calculate the home's tax value crashed and couldn't be brought back up. They tried to use a secondary program, but it had been a while since it was used and wasn't working properly either. This forced the banker to use an outdated book to manually look up the value of the house. Because of this, a new tax value was determined, and we were able to purchase our first home! I suppose this could have just been a coincidence, but I believe it was God working things out for us. On our one-year wedding anniversary, we spent our first night in our new home.

With the purchase of our new home we decided to find a church near-by to attend. Someone recommended one less than a mile from our house, so we gave it a try. It was a small church with very few young people, but we felt so loved there. We kept attending and quickly became very involved. God used this church and these precious people to teach us so much.

Even though we were changing and growing in our faith, we were stuck in several of our old habits. Drinking and smoking cigarettes were my way of coping with stress and depression. I had not been given an official depression diagnosis at that time but looking back, it's clear that's what I was dealing with. I never allowed myself to think deeply. I simply diluted my thoughts and emotions with alcohol almost every night.

In 2005, the back, left side of my head began hurting almost constantly. The pain reminded me of lightning bolts. Nothing would take the pain away. I went to numerous doctors and finally ended up at a neurologist's office. This doctor looked about one hundred and fifty years old and his attitude proved that he was ready to retire. He said the only thing he could do for me was to give me a drug that might help with the pain but would prevent me from having children. Bryan and I had always talked about having a family, but I hadn't allowed that thought to cross my mind very often in the past six years. That train of thought always led to guilt and shame. I did know without doubt, however, that taking a medication that would keep me from having children wasn't even an option for me. When I told the seasoned doctor that I was unwilling to try that medication, he looked at me and said, "Well, you sure are making things difficult for me." I knew right then that he wasn't the doctor that should be treating me.

My brother helped me get an appointment with a revered neurosurgeon at a prominent teaching hospital. Before my appointment, the doctor ordered an MRI, something the other neurologist never even suggested. I was allowed to listen to one of my CDs while lying in the MRI machine. I remember tears rolling down my face as one my favorite worship songs played through the tiny MRI speakers. Although I didn't know what the future held, for the first time I truly understood that God was with me in this difficulty. It was a turning point for me.

After the MRI, we went directly to the neurosurgeon's office. He diagnosed me with Occipital Neuralgia, a nerve condition with an unknown cause. It affects only three out of one hundred thousand people per year. Its sometimes referred to as "The Suicide Disease," because those who have it, never get rid of it and in time, it often becomes more than they can handle. Not only is this condition so rare that most doctors are unaware of it, the treatment options are almost nonexistent. The doctor that diagnosed me connected me with one of his colleagues for treatment. Dr. O was a large man with a dry personality, but it was clear he knew what he was talking about. He was smart, educated, and didn't beat around the bush about what would or would not help me. For months I traveled an hour each way for injections in the base of my head. It was terribly painful and didn't offer much relief from the continuous electrical pain I lived with. When it was clear the shots weren't going to provide relief, Dr. O said the only alternative was to have a Neurostimulator implanted in my head. I remember starring at him blankly, trying to figure out if he was joking. He wasn't.

He told me it was an experimental option that had not been used often for Occipital Neuralgia, but he believed it might offer at least partial relief. He showed me the device that would be implanted in my head, the cord, and battery pack that would be implanted down my back. This option scared me to death. I refused to even consider the implant at first but as the pain worsened, I began to think more about the possibility of having days without this horrible headache. In July 2007, after a year and a half of the continuous pain that had taken over my life, I underwent a lengthy surgery to have the neurostimulator implanted at the bottom left side of my skull, a cord implanted all the way down the left side of my back, and a battery back implanted along my left hip. Part of my head was shaved for the surgery and there were numerous staples down the back of my head and neck. It was a rough recovery. I ended up in the emergency room because I kept throwing up which really isn't good when your head is being held shut with little staples. The doctors there were absolutely amazed by my implant. It was something they had never seen before. They ordered x-rays and CT scans for no real reason, except to see this contraption within my body. Bryan and I joked that I was the "Bionic Woman."

The surgery and recovery allowed me to see an aspect of Bryan I hadn't seen before. He became my caretaker, which is something I hadn't ever needed. I saw a concern in his eyes that blessed my heart tremendously. I couldn't shower for two weeks, so Bryan gave me sponge baths. I couldn't raise my arms for eight weeks, so Bryan helped me get dressed each day. I couldn't pick up anything or strain my neck in any way for three months, so Bryan did all the laundry and housework. This experience caused him to step up in a way that was truly beneficial for our marriage and our future.

All the pain, discomfort, and inconvenience of a neurostimulator implantation were absolutely worth it! When the stimulator was turned on and the settings were correctly configured, the pain disappeared. I was taught how to use the remote control so that any time the pain surfaced, I could alter the settings and get the pain under control. Dr. O explained that the stimulation of the nerve tricks my brain into believing the pain isn't there. It's similar to rubbing your elbow after hitting your "funny bone." The brain focuses on the rubbing instead of the pain. I don't know the specifics of this technology, but I am forever grateful for it and the wise men and women who created it!

15

Getting What I Deserved

THE COMMENTS MADE BY the burnt-out doctor several months prior to my surgery sparked a discussion between Bryan and me. We began thinking about starting a family. We had been married four years, had a cute little home and, with this implant, hopefully I wouldn't be in pain all the time. We knew we wanted to wait until after the surgery but my doctor had suggested I go ahead and stop taking birth control pills a few months before trying to conceive a child. So, for the first time since 1999, I was not preventing pregnancy.

Several weeks into my recovery from the neurostimulator implantation, I noticed that I was a few days late. I secretly took a pregnancy test. And then another. And then another. I couldn't believe it! I was pregnant. A swarm of emotions came over me. I was thrilled but also scared. *What if the abortion damaged me? What if I would be unable to carry this baby?* The thought had never occurred to me before, but now it was one of my greatest concerns. I was in love with the idea of becoming a mommy but also covered with guilt, believing that I didn't deserve to be excited about this pregnancy. Not after my reaction to the last pregnancy. It was very difficult to organize my feelings and thoughts. Prior to that moment, a positive pregnancy test hadn't been something to celebrate. Now, it was a true gift. *What was different this time? I was older. Bryan and I were married. We had a home and jobs. But did any of that make this a gift? Or had a baby been a gift all along, but I just couldn't see it?*

I bought a cute little bib that said, "I love my daddy," and put it around our precious dog's neck. When Bryan saw Mitch, a few minutes later, he was perplexed by what adorned the dog's neck. He picked him up and read it. Watching the news sink in was a sweet moment that I'll never forget. He was going to be a daddy and this time we were both happy about it. We couldn't wait to share the news. We went to the store, bought cute greeting cards and wrote little notes inside that revealed our big news. We drove to see our parents, who still lived on the same street, and gave them the cards. For Bryan's parents this would be their first living grandchild. For my parents, this would be their second. Everyone was thrilled by our announcement.

In the past, being pregnant was accompanied by a world of fear, and disappointment; but soon, after seeing the positive pregnancy test, I began getting used to the idea of pregnancy being a good thing. I was feeling nauseated and had several other pregnancy symptoms. I contacted my doctor and set up my first appointment. I started reading books about pregnancy, trying to eat super healthy, taking folic acid and prenatal vitamins, and began taking better care of my body. My mom shared in my excitement by bringing over a little white teddy bear blanket for her next grandchild. Things were good.

Until the morning I woke up, went to the bathroom, and realized I was bleeding. My heart sunk. I knew instinctively that I had miscarried, but I begged and pleaded with God; hoping that I was wrong. I climbed back into bed with Bryan and told him what was happening. He stayed home from work and we made an appointment to see my doctor. After entering the exam room, I was checked by the doctor, who confirmed the miscarriage.

The next couple of days were so hard. I remember laying on the bed, sobbing. I hated myself so much in those moments. With every single part of me, I believed that I deserved to lose the baby. I believed it was my punishment. I didn't want to talk to anyone. I didn't want to do anything. I was in a pit of depression with no way out. Things began to turn around some when I decided to create something in memory of the baby. I made a small framed picture of baby feet with a poem, along with the date of the miscarriage. It wasn't anything fancy or special, but it was a way for me to memorialize my child, whom we later named Micah. This simple act brought comfort and peace to my heart.

In the days to follow I began preparing my classroom for the upcoming school year. Staff meetings, lesson planning, and trainings filled my days and helped me put the miscarriage behind me. When I did have a few moments to think, I worried over my ability to ever have a baby at all. The miscarriage only added to my fear that the abortion had caused permanent damage and I would not ever be able to carry a baby. I tried to put the thought out of my mind. I prayed that God might give us a child but assumed He wouldn't.

In September of 2007, I bought a digital pregnancy test. I knew I was late and hoped so much that I was pregnant again. I didn't want to take any chances on misreading a test! The digital test made that much easier. I was thrilled to see "pregnant" pop up on the screen of that little stick. I wrapped the test in a box and gave it to Bryan. He shared in my excitement when he opened the box. There was fear, though, that I would miscarry again, so we moved forward with caution.

I went to the doctor soon after because I was cramping and spotting. When the nurse called me back, she took me to a doctor's office instead of a patient room. I was really confused. A doctor I had never met before entered the office and shut the door. He told me that I was having a hysterical pregnancy and needed to understand that there was no way I was pregnant again. I remember looking at him with disbelief and said, "Well, I've already peed in the cup, why don't you do a test yourself and see." He came back a few minutes later and apologized to me. He was wrong. I was pregnant! He explained that some women have bleeding and cramping when the baby is implanting in the uterus and assumed that was probably what I was experiencing. My mind immediately went back to the doctor's office when I was sixteen. *The doctor had said something similar. That must be why I thought I hadn't missed my period. If I was having cramping and bleeding with this baby, I probably did with that one as well.* The doctor ordered bloodwork and asked me to come back in three days for more testing. If the hormone levels were climbing, I could relax and know that everything was progressing as it should. If the levels were dropping or staying the same, I could expect another miscarriage.

Once all the tests were back in, I got the call from my doctor, the one I had been seeing for years, who said that my levels were climbing! "Congratulations!" I remember her saying. "You're going to be a mommy!" The relief that swept over me was beautiful. I had made it further with this pregnancy than the last so maybe there was hope after all.

16

Mommy for the First Time

AS THE PREGNANCY PROGRESSED, I became more and more excited about becoming a mommy. I never allowed myself to fully enjoy the pregnancy, however, because I felt like a fraud. I felt I didn't deserve to have a child after what I had done, and I lived in constant fear that I would miscarry this baby. At five months pregnant, I was having a lot of cramping which prompted the doctor to give me a pelvic exam. She informed me that my cervix was short, most likely caused by the abortion. She was concerned that it could cause premature labor. She warned me of the possibility of having to sew my cervix closed if there were any changes in the coming weeks. Of course, that only added to the fear I already carried. She reexamined me at every appointment but thankfully, my cervix never changed, and I was able to carry the baby to thirty-seven weeks.

While waddling down the hall with my kindergarten class, I felt a warm trickle go down my leg. I freaked out a little inside. *Was I peeing in my pants?* Then it occurred to me, maybe my water had broken! Since the water just kept dripping and now my pants were soaking wet, I knew it was time for this baby to come! It was three weeks early, but the baby was still considered full-term. I yelled out to the playground, asking a fellow teacher to help me, and then I called Bryan. In his shock he asked, "Do I have time to finish my sandwich?" He worked an hour and fifteen minutes away, so it was a reasonable question.

I drove myself home, called the doctor, and then waited on Bryan to get there. I wasn't in any pain, but I couldn't sit still, so I vacuumed the house while I waited. When Bryan arrived, we drove to the hospital and awaited the birth of our first son. After sixteen hours of labor, one of the greatest gifts God has ever given me was placed in my arms. I spent hours just watching Dylan sleep and yawn and wiggle. *How had this amazing little life just been inside of me?*

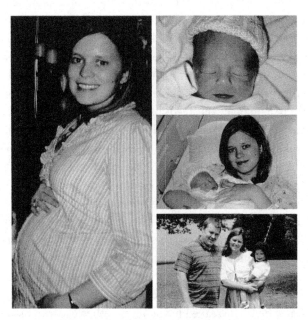

Welcoming our first-born son, Dylan

I was struck with awe at the entire process of pregnancy and birth. If I had ever wondered if my choice to abort was right or wrong, there was no longer any question. That digital "pregnant" on the test led to this magnificent life in my arms. While Bryan went home to walk our dog, I remember laying in the hospital bed, holding my newborn son, and breaking down emotionally. There was no pretending anymore. I knew, without doubt, the abortion had taken the life of another one of *my* children. One just as precious as the one laying in my arms. My pro-life stance was solidified while lying in that hospital bed, concurrently my shame and guilt compounded.

Our first months as a family of three were absolutely wonderful. Bryan and I loved being parents. I stayed home with Dylan until he was three months old and then, even though I hated it tremendously, I took him to daycare and went back to work. The principal moved me to first grade, so I moved my belongings to another classroom, prepared all new lesson plans, and learned a new curriculum. The school year started off well, but I struggled with leaving Dylan at daycare. I pushed through, trying to make the best of the situation.

After Christmas, a new student was placed in my classroom. He was a first grader who had been moved from class to class because of severe behavioral issues. My class was the last first grade classroom he was moved to. He was a sweet child but if something didn't go his way, he turned into someone very different. He was violent and cruel at times. His presence completely changed my classroom, which had previously been a peaceful, loving environment. The behaviors he exhibited only worsened over time. I spoke with the principal and assistant principal repeatedly, but nothing was done to help manage the needs of this child. He had been moved out of all the other first grade classes when his behavior caused too much trouble. But now, there was nowhere else to move him. I began documenting all incidents, keeping track of everything he did. I tried to protect the other students and keep some normalcy in my classroom but there was no doubt, everyone was negatively impacted by the situation. Once he tried to stab another student in the eye with a pencil. He also threw chairs at students on several occasions. I documented these types of destructive behaviors and tried to share this information with the principal, but she never seemed to be interested. I remember telling her, "Someone is going to get hurt. Having him in the classroom is not safe." Even though she saw all the documenta-tion and knew he had wreaked havoc in the other classrooms, she refused to do anything to change the situation.

Around this time Bryan and I decided, after much prayer and dis-cussion, that it was time to move our little family to a new church. It was a very hard choice to make because we loved everyone that attended our little church. But we knew we needed to make the switch to a church with more children. We visited several places and finally settled on a new church home. It was much larger, and the kid's area was incredible. There were kids all over the place! We immediately got plugged in with a small group and got involved with church events. I noticed a change in myself quickly. I was really growing spiritually. I found myself spending a lot of time think-ing about my life as a Christian. I remember driving to work one day and literally asking myself, *"Do I want to go 'all in' on this and be sold out for Jesus? Is that something I want to do? Or do I want to continue going through the motions, never truly walking out this talk?"* I vividly remember the fol-lowing Sunday, standing in the sanctuary's balcony, surrendering my life completely and going "all in" with Jesus!

One afternoon that same week, while my class was lining up to leave the computer lab, the destructive student got angry because he didn't want to leave. This time he decided to take his anger out on me. He ran toward me, pushed me as hard as he could, and knocked me onto the ground. I hadn't been prepared. I didn't know what was about to happen. So, when he pushed me, I was unable to catch myself. I fell hard. I landed right on my tailbone. The kids rushed over to me to help me up. I was embarrassed and tried to make light of the situation but after school, I completed an incident report to formally document what happened.

In the days that followed, I began having a terrible pain in my right leg. I had no idea what was causing the pain, but it wouldn't go away, no matter what remedies I tried. I went to an urgent care to have it checked out. The doctor asked me if I had fallen recently. That's when it hit me. *Yes, I had been knocked down by a student a few days before.* He believed there could be a problem in my back causing the pain in my leg. He suggested I find out who the worker's comp approved doctors were and allow them to help me further.

Filing a worker's comp claim caused a lot of problems for me. The administration treated me poorly and other teachers questioned my pain and need for a doctor. I began to hate going to work and even spent my lunch breaks searching for other jobs on the internet. I felt trapped. All of this, along with the depression, was almost more than I could bear. I typed up scripture verses, taped them all over my desk for encouragement, and played instrumental hymns in my classroom all day.

All I wanted was to be home with my son and never worry over that school again. But that wasn't an option. Bryan and I could never afford for me to be a stay-at-home-mom. As the school year was coming to an end, I submitted a request to be moved to a different school for the following school year. My request was denied. I was stuck, literally. The depression was worsening so I scheduled an appointment and discussed it with my doctor. She diagnosed me with Postpartum Depression and prescribed medication that helped. It didn't change my situation, but it helped me cope with it in a more positive way.

A friend suggested I get in touch with organization that provided free legal advice for teachers in North Carolina. After hearing my story and seeing all my documentation, the doctor's reports, and the transfer denial, the attorney made an appointment to meet with human resources. I'll always be thankful for how hard she fought on my behalf. At the beginning of the summer I was informed that I would begin the 2009–2010 school year at a different elementary school in a kindergarten class. I was elated and relieved!

Throughout the summer the pain in my leg increased and spread up into my lower back. The worker's comp approved doctor suspected a herniated disc or some other issue in my lower back but wanted me to have an MRI. That was impossible because of the neurostimulator I had implanted almost two years prior. A CT scan was ordered but took several weeks to be approved through worker's comp. In the meantime, I began teaching kindergarten at a new school. I was in constant pain, but worker's comp slowed any course of treatment.

One afternoon, while teaching my new kindergarten class, I leaned against a group of desks. The desks slid across the slippery floor, causing me to plop onto a chair and then fall to the floor. It would have been just an embarrassing mishap for most but for someone already dealing with an undiagnosed back issue, it was damaging. The pain I had been experiencing for weeks immediately worsened. I could barely walk or sit. I left school a couple hours later and went directly to the emergency room. A CT scan was done, and I was diagnosed with a fractured spine along with a few other findings that needed further testing. The emergency room doctor gave me shots in my lower back to help ease the pain but insisted I see my worker's comp doctor immediately. I was able to get an appointment within the next day or two. After one look at my CT scan, my doctor took me out of work with an unknown date of return.

I had only worked at the new school for a couple of weeks when I abruptly began staying home full time. I was so confused. I didn't understand. God had worked it out for me to get out of that horrible place and into a new, seemingly wonderful environment but then ripped me away from there. *Why? Was this another punishment?* I was angry but also in so much pain, I knew working wasn't an option.

17

No Wonder You've Been in So Much Pain

IN SEPTEMBER OF 2009, I began life as a stay-at-home-mom. It was only temporary, until my doctor sent me back to work, but I was glad to have the extra time with my baby boy. Days turned into weeks. Weeks turned into months. My doctor prescribed some heavy-duty pain meds and muscle relaxants. It was expected that rest and time would heal my back, but as time went on, it became clear something else must be wrong. Without the ability to have an MRI, I endured test after test. Each one would hopefully determine what was causing the continuous pain. In April of 2010 I was finally diagnosed with an annular tear in the L5S1 disc space, which is essentially a hole in the spinal disc. The fluid from the disc was dripping onto the nerves in my spine. I remember the doctor saying, "No wonder you've been in so much pain!" I was referred to a surgeon and awaited worker's comp approval for surgery to have the disc removed. I was relieved to have a diagnosis after a year of horrific back pain, but the thought of surgery scared me. It had only been two years since my neurostimulator was implanted and I had already been informed that this recovery would be far worse.

On May 9, 2010, exactly one year after being pushed by the student, I underwent spinal fusion surgery and had a cage implanted in my spine where the disc had been. Dylan had just turned two years old the week before. Thankfully, Bryan was able to take six weeks off work to care for Dylan and me. After being in the hospital several days, I began a slow, hard recovery. I had to give myself shots daily, had to use a lifted toilet seat in the bathroom, wore a back brace constantly, and needed help with every single thing I did. Because of all my back pain, we had already taught Dylan to climb into his crib, onto his changing table, into his highchair, and into his car seat. That made it possible for me to take care of him when Bryan went back to work. It was a slow process but, with ridiculous amounts of physical therapy, I eventually regained the ability to take care of myself and Dylan. I wasn't allowed to pick him up though, which was heartbreaking for me.

The surgeon was never pleased with my recovery, so he continued to keep me out of work. Being home with Dylan became the new norm for our family and I really enjoyed being a stay-at-home-mom. Once fall rolled around and I was able to do more physically, I began attending Tuesday morning Women's Bible studies at church and a mom's group on Thursday mornings. Being in God's Word and surrounding myself with godly women had a huge impact on my walk with Jesus. My faith grew by leaps and bounds during this season of my life. I still dealt with a whole lot of pain and had to take pain pills non-stop, but it was a sweet time.

In October of 2010, I decided to think of one thing each day in November that I was grateful for. I remember talking with Bryan about this idea and he asked, "Do you really think you can think of thirty things?" It was a good question; I had wondered the same thing. This thought challenged me, and I made it my goal to find reasons to be thankful each day of November. I ended up being pleasantly surprised by how easy this task was. I was really moved by the entire experience and decided to start 2011 with a new challenge . . . to write a blog sharing one thing I was grateful for everyday of 2011. I began writing the blog January 1, 2011.

Early in 2011, we found out I was pregnant with our second son. It was somewhat scary because of all that my body had been through in 2010, but we were thrilled. The pregnancy was hard on my body though. I was hospitalized ten weeks into the pregnancy because of Hyperemesis Gravidarum, which is severe nausea, vomiting, weight loss, and dehydration. This experience was eerily like my pregnancy at sixteen. The back pain increased substantially as the pregnancy progressed, and I did my best to endure the pain without taking heavy pain killers. I spent a lot of time thinking about the baby I was carrying. I read everything I could about his development and what was happening inside my womb. I was in awe of what God was doing within me.

I continued writing my blog, throughout the winter and spring. My simple, surface level thankfulness began to morph into thought-provoking, deeper gratitude. It must have been evident to my readers as well because I was asked to be a contributor for a Christian magazine. I would be writing an article in each issue. I was so humbled and honored to be asked to share my thoughts and the things God was teaching me in a magazine. To think that God might use my words amazed me! Of course, the enemy continually used my past choices to try and deter me from following through with this task. He never stopped condemning me for the abortion or all the junk that followed it. As I wrote the words for each issue of the publication, I felt like an imposter. Always believing that if anyone really knew my past, they wouldn't let me type another word.

In the summer of 2011, I received a call alerting me that my dad had been in a car accident and was being airlifted to a local hospital. I rushed to the hospital and found him laying on a stretcher, covered in blood, missing several teeth, wearing a neck brace and other straps to keep him from moving. His appearance frightened me. I just had to pray over him, out loud, right there in the middle of the emergency room. He had been driving when his truck flipped. The EMS workers found him hanging out of the back windshield. He was lucky to be alive. I stayed with him the rest of the day and went back first thing the next morning. Seeing him this way made an impression on my heart. He was so fragile, so human. Miraculously, his injuries were minimal, and he slowly recovered. I'll never forget sitting beside his hospital bed when he poured out his heart to me, apologizing for the things that occurred during my childhood. I hadn't expected to ever hear an apology and didn't realize how much I needed to hear those sincere words. In that moment, I was so incredibly grateful that God had given me the ability to love my dad even through all the difficulty and uncertainty. Our relationship hadn't been perfect, but I never gave up on him and I considered that an incredible blessing. Talking openly with my dad in that hospital room and hearing the heartfelt thoughts of a man who had so many regrets, enlarged my heart toward him and toward people in general. We're all a mess, just trying to do the best we can in this crazy life. Sometimes we're on top of the world and sometimes, we fall flat on our faces. I thanked God for forgiveness and grace. I thanked Him for enabling me to stay connected to my father through it all and teaching me how to see others as He does, with compassion and love.

The end of my pregnancy was tough. The back pain was tremendous. It had been a year and a half since my surgery, but my pain was worse than ever. We prayed and prayed for this child to be born at thirty-seven weeks, just like his older brother was. I needed relief physically but also, Bryan's grandfather's health was declining quickly, and we wanted the chance to visit him once more in Pennsylvania. We asked our small group to join us in that prayer one Sunday morning before attending the worship service. They gathered around us and prayed that God might work things out so we could visit Poppop once more. After the prayer we walked to the sanctuary. Bryan sat down in a pew and I went to the restroom. I was about to head back to my seat, when I felt my water break. I rushed into the sanctuary to tell Bryan. He couldn't believe it. He thought I was joking, since we had just been praying for this! Thankfully, once again, the water was only a trickle, but I definitely wasn't joking! We picked up Dylan from his Sunday school class and headed home. Bryan's parents arrived to watch Dylan and we rushed to the hospital. I was in complete awe of God's answer to our prayers.

After eighteen hours of labor, we welcomed Evan into the world. He was absolutely precious. His presence was accompanied by peace and love and so much joy. I couldn't believe God would bless me with another perfect little boy. All the while, in the back of my mind, I was scolding myself repeatedly and believed I would never be the mother these boys needed. *Since I chose to kill my first child, I don't deserve to have these boys or the love that they would bring into my life.* Fear and worry manifested in my heart and kept me from truly enjoying the blessings God had given me.

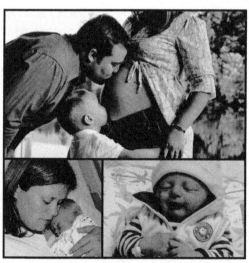

A new addition to our family, our second son, Evan

18

Time is Marching On

JUST AS WE HAD prayed for with our church family, we were able to visit Poppop in Pennsylvania once more when Evan was just three weeks old. It was a sweet visit for all of us even though we knew it was the last time we'd see him in this life. Poppop passed away a couple of weeks later. The incredible answers to prayer didn't go unnoticed by either of us. The realization that God was working things out for us, started to really settle in.

The year came to an end and I completed the three hundred and sixty fifth day of my blog, "A Year of Gratitude." I had actually thought of three hundred and sixty-five reasons to be grateful. The experience had a beautiful impact on my life. Throughout the year, I began thinking in a different way. I no longer had to search for things I was thankful for. Now, I was simply grateful. At any moment, I could share numerous reasons for gratitude. My mind shifted tremendously over those twelve months. I loved the change in my thinking, so I decided not to end the blog. Instead, I changed the title to "A Life of Gratitude," and committed to continue writing as God prompted my heart to do so.

I continued to deal with back pain and worker's comp while mothering a three-year-old and an infant. It was physically demanding, but I enjoyed being home with my babies. I often spent time looking back on those days in my first-grade classroom, searching on the internet for possible jobs, fearing I would be stuck in that school forever. *Look at what God had done.* Not only had He removed me from that situation, but He had completely transformed my life. I was now a stay-at-home mom, something we could have never, ever done on our own.

My doctors continued to be concerned by my pain and lack of recovery. The worker's comp case manager began to think I was faking my pain so I could stay out of work. So, a barrage of medical tests were performed to see the status of my spine. A series of functionality tests and psychological tests were completed as well, to determine my motives and abilities. Of course, everything with a worker's comp takes weeks to arrange and the appointments are scheduled weeks out, so I continued happily with my life as a stay at home mom.

When Dylan turned four in May of 2012, Bryan and I began to contemplate homeschooling. I had never even considered homeschooling our children. In fact, as a teacher, I had mostly looked down on folks who homeschooled their children, even though I really knew nothing about it. Dylan was already reading, and I knew, as a former kindergarten teacher, that he was ready for school. Bryan and I decided to each spend a month praying separately about the topic. We also made pros/cons lists as we prayed. When the month was up, we discussed the topic thoroughly, and even though I could be sent back to work at any time, we believed God wanted us to step out in faith and homeschool our son.

In August of 2012, I had a very difficult time with stomach pain. It was excruciating. After several tests and a few days in the hospital, it was determined that I needed my gallbladder removed. So, I underwent my third surgery in two years. It was such a gift, however. As soon as I woke up, the pain I had been enduring was gone and I was able to get back to my life after a few days of rest and healing. It was so easy to see God throughout the situation. I was never fearful or worried. He was with me the entire time.

In September of 2012, we began our homeschooling journey. Each afternoon, while Evan napped, Dylan and I would complete his kindergarten work. He grew by leaps and bounds. It was clear that we had made the right choice to start kindergarten at four years old. He loved to read and enjoyed learning! Our choice to homeschool wasn't fully embraced by everyone in our lives at first. They didn't say much but it was clear they were unsure about our decision. After several months, however, they began to see the power of moving at a child's own pace and were impressed by the progress Dylan was making.

Life moved on and I continued to deal with back and hip pain. In October 2012, one of many tests involved a spinal tap. During a spinal tap, a needle is placed within the fluid-filled space that surrounds your spinal cord. A passage is created where the spinal fluid can leak out, which inevitably changes the fluid pressure around your brain and spinal cord. If enough of the fluid leaks out, or it doesn't heal correctly, a spinal headache can occur, which is what happened to me. Typically, a blood patch will close the hole and the headache will go away. The headache I endured was followed by three failed blood patches. It became clear that I was dealing with something more significant. Every time I sat up or stood straight for more than a couple of minutes, I got violently ill. I ended up in the emergency room several times and then sent back to my living room couch, where I laid flat, all day, for four weeks. We witnessed the love and concern of the church so profoundly during these weeks. Meals were brought in, laundry was washed and folded, errands were run, and even a "girl's night in" was arranged.

The doctor who performed the test which led to this month-long nightmare, refused to help me any further and "lost" my medical record. I was beginning to lose hope that I would ever feel better, but I saw God's handiwork all over this situation. Eventually, a neurologist that went to the church we attended was able to see me on a Saturday morning. He determined that the leak in my spinal column may have already healed but the blood vessels and nerves in my head were extremely aggravated and causing the horrible pain I continued to have. He administered a shot which gave me some immediate relief and then prescribed two migraine medications to take every two hours to try to get the pain under control. I also had emergency shots to give myself in case the pain worsened again. Believe it or not, the very next day I was able to go to a marriage conference at church with Bryan. Despite there being very little hope in sight, I had been praying for two weeks that I would feel well enough to attend and God answered my prayer!

It took a few months for me to fully recover from that painful experience. After slowly reducing the dosage over a two-year period, I was able to wean myself off the medication that gave me my life back. It was truly a gift from the Lord.

19

The Beauty of Transparency

AS LIFE MARCHED ON, I grew closer and closer to Jesus. I had seen Him so profoundly through both ordeals with my gallbladder and the spinal headache. I spent time with Him daily, enjoyed teaching my sons about Him, and volunteered as often as I could at church. I was asked to speak at the mom's group I attended, sharing God's faithfulness in my life and the things He had been teaching me. Each "Life of Gratitude" blog post was being read by hundreds of people from several different countries. I was getting comments and messages from people all over the world, telling me how much the blog encouraged them and inspired them to look for things to be grateful for in their own lives. Even though I was overwhelmed by God's goodness, I struggled consistently with feeling like a fraud. I had a vile, ugly, disgustingly dark secret festering inside of me. I had barely discussed it with anyone, even Bryan. I lived in constant fear that, somehow, my secret would be revealed, and everyone would see me as the imposter I believed I was.

In 2012, I came across a blog post written by someone I had recently met. As I read the post, I could barely believe my eyes. She was sharing about an abortion she had at seventeen years old. While reading Melissa's story, my heart ached for her and for myself. Our stories were very similar in some ways but very different in other ways. I couldn't stop wondering, *how in the world was she able to share this so openly? Didn't she feel the shame and guilt I felt?*

After rereading Melissa's post numerous times, I sent her a text message asking if we could get together later in the week to discuss something.

I was afraid to even type the words explaining what I wanted to talk about, but I believe she knew. We met a few days later and while our children played, I opened up to her. For the first time ever, I told the entire story of the abortion I had when I was sixteen years old. Her response was one of acceptance and love. I asked her how she was able to openly share and then I said with certainty, "I will never be able to share my story the way you did."

She explained that she had previously done a post-abortive Bible study which had truly changed her life. *Gosh, I had never even thought about a post-abortive Bible study. I didn't even know that existed.* The more I thought about it, the more I realized, I had never even really talked to God about this topic. I had been growing in my faith and even sharing that faith with others but had never allowed God into this part of my past. God was using this friend and her story to help me find more of Him, even in the darkest part of my life.

She offered to get a copy of the study for me from the local pregnancy care center. Once she did, we went through the study together. It was a grueling process. I had buried so many of my memories and emotions. Drudging it all up was painful. The study went into great detail, encouraging me to really face the choice I made and the impact it had on me and others in my life. It also suggested I give my preborn baby a name, which wasn't an easy thing to do, especially knowing I was the one who allowed this child's life to be taken. God gave me the strength and courage, however, to name my child Taylor, which could be for a boy or a girl. Picking a name ended up being a very powerful. It gave the baby an identity instead of it remaining a statistic. The study also allowed me to experience what being the beneficiary of forgiveness truly feels like. I knew God had forgiven me, but I had not wholly accepted that forgiveness. Keeping the abortion hidden deep in my soul had been causing me so much more pain and doubt than I had ever realized. This study released the enemy's grip on this area of my life, at least in part.

As the eight-week study progressed, I knew I needed to discuss it with Bryan. He didn't know I had shared my story with this friend and had no idea I was seeking forgiveness and healing through a Bible study. A movie telling the story of a survivor of a failed abortion had recently been released and I suggested we watch it. When the movie ended, for the first time in thirteen years, Bryan and I talked about the baby we aborted. I remember feeling as though a ton of weight was being lifted off my chest. I laid my head on his shoulder and sobbed. It was awkward but wonderful to recognize, out loud, the baby who had been our secret for so long.

At the end of the study the author suggested doing something in honor of the aborted child. No one knew I was doing this study because no one knew abortion was a part of my past so, I was unsure of what to do or how to do it. Around that time, our family participated in a service project with our small group. The project had been planned months before by a member of our group. We would be cleaning up the garden area at our local pregnancy care center. When we arrived and I saw the garden, I could barely believe my eyes. The garden was called, "A Memorial Garden for the Unborn." God had been orchestrating this for me because He cared about the healing journey I was on. He gave me the perfect opportunity to silently honor the child that would have been twelve years old at the time. I will never forget sitting beside a flower bed, planting beautiful pansies. With each one I planted; more tears fell. I had my back turned to the rest of the group, so no one saw the highly emotional gardening experience. For the first time, I physically acknowledged the life I ended. There was so much power in that simple act.

The last day Melissa and I met to discuss the Bible study, I remember telling her that even though God had used the experience to help me accept His forgiveness, I still didn't think I could ever tell anyone what I had done. She assured me I didn't have to if I didn't want to. But she also said, "In time God may use your story, you never know." I highly doubted it, since I had absolutely no plans of sharing this secret. Ever.

20

The Transition

ONCE I COMPLETED THE Post-Abortive Bible Study, I tucked it away on my bookshelf and put the experience behind me. I was busy with life as a mom and wife. I continued to struggle with back pain, but now more areas of my body were affected. My upper back, neck, and ribcage bothered me most of the time. My doctors didn't understand where all the pain was coming from. For the most part, they tried to treat my symptoms, never seeking out the cause.

Over a year earlier, we put our little home on the market. It had been the perfect place for us while we had our first child, but we knew we wanted to have at least three children and there just wasn't room. Plus, the yard was too small for the kids to play in and there weren't any other children in the neighborhood. Selling the house was a long, slow process. The market was in bad shape and there were countless houses for sale in our area. We had it listed for about as low as we could, but we couldn't really compete with the other sellers in our area. It felt as if the house would never sell.

The waiting and wondering during this time were hard. I questioned myself, God, and everything else. I spent a lot of time in prayer and I knew God was telling me that he had something big in store for us. My worker's comp case would hopefully settle soon and could help us purchase a new home. *It all made sense, so why wasn't it happening?* While the house was listed on the market, I had access to a website showing all the houses for sale in our area. I spent many hours searching for the perfect house for us. I came across a beautiful white house with four bedrooms, three baths, and an office we could use as a schoolroom. I drove by the house and fell in love with the neighborhood. The house was in a cul-de-sac and sat beside a little pond. It seemed perfect. I began to drive by, once a week or so, to pray over the house. I knew this was our house, but we weren't able to move into it yet. God used this experience to teach me so much about waiting and letting Him lead. I learned to really listen for His voice and stop questioning what I hear. I began to refer to this house, in my own mind at least, as our Promised Land. God had promised this land to us but the journey to get there was long.

The back pain continued, and my endless doctor appointments did as well. I went to every appointment feeling as if the doctor held my fate in his hands. At any time, he could decide to send me back to work. Most of the time he was very compassionate toward me, but eventually seemed to get tired of the continuous pain he couldn't find a cause for. He began to insinuate that I was making it up. It was disheartening but since it was a worker's comp case, I couldn't just switch doctors. At one appointment, the case worker made the doctor fill out a form stating my work status. As Bryan and I sat in the doctor's office, waiting to hear his decision, I repeated Isaiah 43:13 over and over in my head. "I am the Lord your God, who takes hold of your right hand and says, do not fear, I will help you."

There was no way I could go back to teaching kindergarten. The energy level needed, and the hours spent on my feet, just weren't possible with the pain I endured daily. The thought of being sent back to work terrified me because I had absolutely no say in it.

The doctor looked up and said, "I just don't see any medical reason you can't go back to work." I tried to argue with him, telling him all my valid reasons, but he didn't want to hear it. He left the room to complete the paperwork. I looked at Bryan with disbelief, but we resolved that we would trust God, no matter what. The doctor returned and told us to follow him up to the nurse's station to get a copy of the paperwork. Tears streamed down my face as I walked slowly behind him. Bryan's right hand was clenching my left.

"I am the Lord your God, who takes hold of your right hand and says, do not fear, I will help you," played over and over in my head. We got to the desk, the nurse made a copy of the form and handed it to me. I looked at it and handed it to Bryan. He looked closely. Our eyes turned toward each other. *Were we reading this correctly?* The doctor, who had just said I was returning to work, had signed the paper stating that I would never be returning to work.

My first thought was to pretend I didn't notice. *Maybe if we didn't draw any attention to it, he wouldn't see his mistake.* But this was still a worker's comp case, so the case worker got a copy as well. She assured me it was a mix up and it would get worked out. At that moment, I didn't care. At least this had given me a few more days before returning to work. Several days later the case worker called to say the doctor decided to stick with his accidental decision to keep me out of work. It was an error on his part, but his pride wouldn't let him admit that.

This was incredible. God had done something huge! That doctor said with absolute certainty that I would be returning to work because he didn't believe I was in any real pain. He was adamant. He didn't even want to hear my arguments. But God had helped me, just as Isaiah 43:13 said He would. He took hold of my right hand and worked things out in a way that only He could. I wouldn't be going back to teaching, ever. This decision began to bring some closure to my worker's comp case, which had been painfully slow, but there was finally a light at the end of the tunnel.

In November 2013 our little house finally went under contract, after being on the market for two and a half years. The worker's comp case hadn't been finalized yet, so we needed to wait to put an offer on a new home. My mom and stepdad offered for us to live with them until the case closed.

At that time, the white house beside the pond was still for sale. I had been driving by it consistently for a year now. I still believed this was our Promised Land and that this would be the last leg of our journey. Bryan thought I was silly. He didn't think we would ever have a house as nice as that one. He was skeptical and didn't want me to get my hopes up. I was tempted to get angry but instead, I remembered a verse from Luke chapter two that says, "Mary treasured up all of these things and pondered them in her heart." I didn't want to get discouraged, so I decided to treasure what God was telling me and keep the thoughts to myself. I believed Him, even if it made no sense to other people.

A month before Christmas we moved out of our little house, put most of our belongings in storage, and moved into my mom's house. I was once again sleeping in the bedroom I had slept in growing up. My children were sleeping in the room next to mine. It was odd. I was grateful to my parents for allowing us to live there but I honestly felt out of place. Not because of anyone or anything specific, but because I never imagined I would end up living with my parents again, especially with my husband and two small children.

In the days leading up to Christmas, I discovered that the house I had my heart set on was no longer available. I was devastated. I had basically decorated the entire house in my mind and had spent hours daydreaming of our life within those walls. I also felt embarrassed. *I thought I heard God so clearly. I believed Him and trusted that He would come through. But what now?*

The day before Bryan's birthday in 2014, I had a feeling that I was pregnant. I went to the store, bought a test, and planned to take it first thing in the morning the next day. Sure enough, on Bryan's thirty-third birthday, I found out I was expecting baby number three. I wrapped the test up like a birthday present and gave it to him a few hours later. He was shocked, to say the least. We dressed the boys up in "Big Brother" t-shirts and throughout the day our families figured out the big news.

This wasn't at all what we had planned. We were still living in my mom's house with no definite plans for a new house or the settlement. I was thrilled to be expecting another baby, but I couldn't shake the irony of the situation. Here I was, living at my mom's house, finding out about an unexpected pregnancy. The similarities didn't end there. Pretty soon I was terribly sick again. I couldn't keep anything down and felt miserable all the time. I was laying in the same bed I laid in at sixteen years old. My mom would check on me now and then and thankfully, she cared for the boys while I rested. There were several days I didn't get up until almost dinner time. Time seemed to creep by but soon I was feeling some better.

At last, my worker's comp case came to an end in April. At the same time, Bryan received an unexpected job offer which paid substantially more than his previous position. We quickly began looking for our next home. We visited numerous homes, but I wasn't happy with any of them. None of them were the one I believed was ours. One morning, as I scanned all the available homes on the website, I saw it. The white house beside the pond was back on the market! Bryan and I went to check it out, along with a few others. We found two we really liked. The white house and another one a few miles away from it. The other house had a much bigger yard which caused us to go back and forth between the houses but in the end, we put an offer on the little white house beside the pond. We were quickly under contract and the plans for moving in began.

On May 1, Dylan's sixth birthday, we found out the gender of our third baby. Dylan had been so excited, he asked to find out the gender on his birthday and have a "gender reveal party." So, after the appointment, we took the closed envelope to a nearby grocery store and had the clerk insert the correct color of balloons in a big box. None of us knew the gender because we had asked the ultrasound technician to write it down and place it in the envelope. The reveal party was a lot of fun and we were all incredibly excited to see pink balloons pop up from the decorated box.

As our move-in date grew closer, tension in my mom's house began to build. There were arguments and hurtful things said. We were ready to move into our home and my parents were probably ready for that as well. It wasn't an ideal situation any longer. With two days left before closing on our house, I found a letter laying on the kitchen table, addressed to me. Bryan was at work and the kids wanted to play outside, so I got them settled with their bikes and sidewalk chalk before I opened the envelope.

I began reading the note and immediately felt sick to my stomach. It was several pages long and filled with belittling comments. Situations and conversations from my entire life were being thrown in my face, including particular things I said when I was a kid and an argument my mom and I had over my wedding invitations. Tears trickled down my cheeks. I couldn't understand why my mom and stepdad would even write a letter like this. It wasn't like them. *Did they believe this would dissolve the tension in the house?* I kept reading and then I saw it. The worst paragraph in the whole letter. It was a paragraph focused entirely on the abortion. We had never discussed it, in all those years, and now they were using it to shame me. It cut me to the core. As I finished reading the letter, I discovered we were being kicked out. I was six months pregnant, with two small, very confused little boys, and I had nowhere to go.

I called Bryan while the kids still played in the driveway. I was hysterical. He couldn't understand me through my frantic tears. I was able to calm myself enough to tell him about the letter. He immediately took on a role I hadn't seen before. He would protect me at all costs and didn't want me to cry one more tear over this. He left within minutes of our phone call and I began to pack our stuff. He worked an hour and a half away, so I made a lot of progress while I waited on him. I cried and cried as I packed our bags. I didn't want to tell the kids what was happening, but what choice did I have? I was gentle with my words, as not to say hurtful things about their grandparents. The boys helped me pack and make the beds. They hauled trash bags full of clothes downstairs and lugged their toys to the kitchen and placed them in boxes.

I looked out the kitchen window, and there he was, like a superhero arriving to save the day. Bryan pulled into the driveway in a moving truck. He was making sure we wouldn't have come back for anything. He ran inside and pulled me close. He knew how broken my heart was. He let me cry on his shoulder for a few minutes and then we began a long afternoon of packing and moving. The four of us had been living with my parents for seven months. We had been purchasing things for our new home, the kids had received lots of Christmas gifts, and I had been given several things from my grandparent's home. We had accumulated a lot. This move was abrupt, so we had no one to help us and I was six months pregnant, so I wasn't much help with the heavy stuff. Thankfully, Bryan's parents left work and came to assist us.

When we finally got everything packed up, we drove the truck down the street to Bryan's parent's house. They didn't have empty bedrooms for us to stay in for long, but thankfully we only needed to stay two nights. I barely slept because of my usual pain and the discomforts of pregnancy, but also, my heart was grief-stricken. *How could my mother do this to me and my children? We only needed to stay two more nights. Were they just being spiteful?* I read and reread the letter, trying to make sense of it. I couldn't believe it, no matter how many times my eyes skimmed the page. I felt terribly rejected and unwanted. I felt as though my parent's love was entirely conditional and they had been keeping a record of wrongs my entire life. I didn't even understand why they kicked us out. I just knew that things would never be the same.

Our White House Beside the Pond

On June 4, 2014 we closed on our new home and began moving into our Promised Land. We celebrated our tenth wedding anniversary on June 5th. The little white house beside the pond was ours and it had never felt so good to be home. God's grace carried us through the wilderness and into our Promised Land. The journey was long and unpleasant at times, but it was also purposeful. God used this experience to prove Himself to us and it would become a time we would recall often to remind us of His faithfulness.

21

Surprise!

IN THE WEEKS AND months that followed, things did not improve with my parents. They sent email after email with more hateful comments. Being pregnant, this type of treatment was particularly unhealthy for me. The stress caused me to begin contracting and dilating very early. I had to rest and lay around as much as possible until the baby reached thirty-seven weeks.

One of the emails I received from my mother, informed me that she had taken copies of the letter and given them to Bryan's family and several other family members. She stressed how shocked everyone was with my behavior and how disappointed everyone was in me. I'll never understand the purpose behind sharing the letter with anyone. It honestly wouldn't have mattered much except for *that one thing* I never wanted anyone to find out about. Knowing that my mother used the letter to tell so many people about a very dark, painful time in my life, cut my heart in two. *She hadn't even spoken to me about it since it happened and now, she was telling anyone that would listen. What was the point in that?*

I talked often with Melissa, my friend who had led me through the post-abortive Bible study. She understood my frustration and shame better than anyone. She validated my feelings and agreed that telling folks about the abortion was too far. I had done my best to be prayerful and kind in my responses to those emails. I had tried to let it go and make the best of a terrible situation. I had believed that things would get better and this would all go away. But this was too far. I had to protect myself and my family by putting some boundaries in place. As hard as it was to do, I blocked all communication from my mom.

I spent a lot of time praying over this situation. I was emotionally and physically exhausted, but God used this difficult experience to speak directly to my soul. He revealed my fear of abandonment and rejection and helped me to better understand the source of it. With His help, I began to accept being deserted by my father as a child and rejected by mother as an adult. He exposed my obsession with the opinion others had of me. He also supernaturally eased the pain of my secret being exposed by my own mother. I began to care less and less that so many people had read about the abortion, but I never wanted to be around them again. I knew the shame would smoother me if I had to look them in the eye.

As the birth of our third child drew near, I tried to smooth things out with my mom and decided to let her know when I went into labor. This would be her first granddaughter and I just didn't have the heart to keep her from being at the hospital when she was born.

In mid-September my doctor decided to induce labor because of my intense back pain. As we waited in the hospital room, for our daughter to enter the world, my mom, dad, and stepmom waited in the waiting room. Once we knew the baby would be born soon, Bryan's parents brought our boys to the hospital. I only had to push three times and out came our sweet baby. The doctor proudly stated, "It's a boy!"

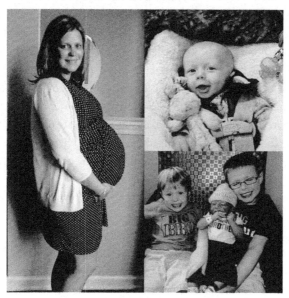

A Surprise Addition to Our Family, Tyson

I looked at her, in complete shock, and said, "It's a what?" She said nonchalantly, "It's a boy." I looked at Bryan and he looked at me. I couldn't make sense of what she was saying. *I thought we were having a girl. Hadn't we sold all the blue items we used with our two older boys at a consignment sale and bought tons of pink items to replace them? We had a purple nursery and frilly hair bows, adorable dresses and socks with lace around the top, didn't we?*

The nurses quickly caught on to our shock and said, "Oh no! They were told they were having a girl!" The doctor looked surprised and showed us the proof that this was, indeed, a little boy. They laid him on my chest and even though I was in complete shock, my heart leapt with joy as my child opened his eyes and looked at me. I fell instantly in love with him. After a few minutes, the nurses took him over to weigh and measure him. As I watched him from a distance, my heart began to ache. I really couldn't believe that in 2014, an ultrasound technician could get the gender of a baby wrong!

Bryan called his parents to let them know the crazy news. We needed them to prepare the boys to meet their brother, instead of a sister. We knew they would be upset because they had been so thrilled with the thought of having a baby girl in our family. When they arrived with the kids, my dad met them in the hallway where he learned the shocking news. As he walked back into the waiting room, his face was apparently as white as a ghost. Everyone in the room thought something terrible had happened. He explained that I had given birth to a little boy but that we were both doing well.

When Dylan and Evan entered the room, they were visibly upset. They were in shock too. But, as soon as they snuggled beside me on the bed and looked at their new brother, they "oooo'd and awww'd" and quickly forgot about the sister they thought they wanted. They were especially happy that their pirate themed bathroom wouldn't have to change! They took turns holding the baby and talked about the things they would teach him and the adventures they would allow him to tag along on.

Over the next hour or two, our parents took turns coming in the room to meet their newest grandson. No one could believe it, but everyone instantly fell in love with this little guy. When I saw my dad enter the room, I broke into tears. I felt like I had let everyone down. I knew how excited they had all been for a baby girl. Seeing my dad caused so many emotions within me and I couldn't contain it. I was suddenly so worried that this little boy would think no one wanted him. I moved from being in shock to being broken-hearted because I wasn't prepared for him. I was worried that he would grow up believing his birth was a disappointment. Nothing could be farther from the truth, but because of the feelings of abandonment and disappointment I dealt with as a child, my heart was filled with concern for this precious boy. The nurses could see the pain on my face. They went on a search through the hospital to find a blue hat and a blue blanket for this sweet one to wear. I think it was more for me, because they could see how my heart ached.

That night, Bryan ran out to get some boy outfits and blankets, since everything we had brought with us was pink. He came back with a onesie that said, "Born Rebel." It was perfect! As I dressed him in that little onesie, I was filled with gratitude. This special little one wasn't what I had expected but he was precious. I could already tell how sweet and snuggly he would be and as I looked back over the eventful day, I realized that this was the best surprise Bryan and I would ever receive.

We didn't have a boy's name picked out because we had spent the past five months thinking we were having a girl. So, Bryan and I spent hours and hours searching for the perfect name for our new son. We didn't want him to go even twenty-four hours without his own special name. We didn't have anything else for him, but we could give him a name! This proved to be a difficult task but in the early morning hours, after being awake all night, we decided on the name Tyson. It means "explosive" or "fiery and high spirit!" This strong name was perfect for our surprise who made such an explosive entrance into our family!

When we arrived home, the nursery was already painted blue. Bryan had hired painters to come while I was still in the hospital. The days to follow were filled with packing up girly clothes and accessories, returning items that still had the tags, and stocking up on boy stuff. Folks came out of the woodwork with gifts containing boy clothes, blue blankets, blue burp cloths, blue towels, and anything else they thought we might need. Within a week, all evidence of pink and purple was gone, and the nursery obviously belonged to a boy. It became very clear that God cared about the intimate details of my life. He provided everything we needed for Tyson but also, most of what we wanted. He knew how much it meant to me to have a nursery for a little boy so, He provided everything we needed, in just a few days! We could have used the pink burp cloths, but God provided everything in blue and green, simply because He knew how much it meant to me.

To be honest, those days were hard for me. I had spent a lot of time preparing for a daughter; washing and drying pink dresses, painting the letters for her name to hang on the wall, making hairbows, folding purple towels, and packing a polka dotted diaper bag. I had also spent a lot of hours daydreaming of dance classes, fingernail painting, and doll houses. Others could laugh about our big surprise, but I couldn't, at least not for a while.

When you've spent months bonding with a child, calling it by name, decorating a room, buying clothes, and celebrating with friends and family, you feel like you know the child before it's even born. When that child is born and is a different gender, it feels as if the child you knew has gone missing. In a matter of seconds, she simply ceased to exist. As soon as the baby is placed in your arms, however, there is also an instant love for the newborn, even though he wasn't who you expected. My heart immediately filled with love for Tyson. I was so worried about him. I felt badly that I hadn't prepared for him, that I hadn't "bonded" with him, that I hadn't celebrated him. So many times, my eyes flooded with tears because I felt like I lost the girl I had been dreaming of and, at the same time, I let down this precious boy God had given me. The emotions were strong and so confusing, not to mention they were laced with hormones! I had a dream ripped right out of my heart while a new one was placed in my arms. It was indescribable loss and instant love . . . all at once.

I spent night after night rocking this precious boy, calling out to Jesus with all my emotions. I began to realize that the heart and mind are seriously complex. I experienced happiness and sadness at the same time. I felt grateful while also feeling disappointed. I felt full of love while also feeling like something was missing. One night, while rocking my baby, my head was filled with thoughts of the abortion I had so many years ago. I began to convince myself that God was using this situation to laugh at me and teach me some sort of lesson. I cried out to Him, *"Why did you do this to me? I would have been perfectly fine having another boy, I love my boys, but why did it have to be such a shocking experience?"* As I rocked that wooden chair, holding this precious boy, with tears streaming down my face, I heard my Father say, "I didn't do this to you. I did it for you." The voice had been almost audible. It struck me and comforted me all at once. *What did that mean?*

Over the next couple of months, God taught me many things through His Word, through friends and family's comments, and through those hours rocking my baby boy in the night. I learned that this had been no surprise to God. *This was no mistake!* Psalm 139:13–16 says, "For You created my inmost being, You knit me together in my mother's womb. I praise You because I am fearfully and wonderfully made; Your works are wonderful; I know that full well. My frame was not hidden from You when I was made in the secret place. When I was woven together in the depths of the earth, Your eyes saw my unformed body. All the days ordained for me were written in Your book before one of them came to be." Every single day of my pregnancy, my God knew that we had a big surprise in store. He created this child to be a boy and placed him in our family on purpose. He had known Tyson's identity all along and just because I didn't know the truth about Tyson, didn't make it any less true.

God taught me that a person's identity is given by Him alone. What the world thinks of us and how we are perceived has no effect on who He created us to be. God was using Tyson to change my life and he was only a few months old. I began to truly understand that my identity is in Christ. Not in my childhood, not in the abortion I had at sixteen, not in my relationship with Bryan, not in my successes or my failures, not in other's opinions of me, and not in my performance as a wife and mother. Just like Tyson, even if no one knew who I really was or even if they thought the worst about me, it didn't change a thing. *I am God's daughter. Loved and known by the One who created me. Forgiven and cherished by the One who died for me. Chosen and blessed by the One who walks with me daily.*

God really had done this *for* me. Without this shocking time in my life, I may have never truly understood that God is the creator of all life and the giver of my identity. I discovered who I was and my value. I began to truly believe that I was loved, regardless of what I had done in the past.

22

Tearing Down the Walls

LIFE WAS DIFFERENT WITH three children, but Bryan and I were adapting well. I was learning so many things in my time alone with the Lord and became incredibly grateful to be given the opportunity to raise another son for God's Kingdom. *The world definitely needs more Godly men!* My relationship with my mom and stepdad continued to be a trying situation. God had been teaching me about my identity in Christ and for the first time, the information was making the eighteen-inch journey from head to my heart. But the struggle with my mom threatened to rip away all that God had taught me. I had to set boundaries once again and many months went by without us seeing or talking to each other. While it wasn't apparent to us at the time, God was working in their lives too. Situations, circumstances, and conversations were causing their hearts, and ours, to be softened, and perspectives to change. In time, apologies were made, and mercy was given. We began to spend some time together and then eventually, by God's grace, our relationship became stronger than it ever had been before. He restores what is broken, when we allow Him to.

A few months after Tyson was born, Bryan and I both began desiring more in our walk with God. As much as we loved our church, we just didn't feel as though we were continuing to grow as Christ Followers. We began attending a new church that would end up being an incredible blessing for our family. Within just a couple of months of finding this church, I experienced a miracle there. On January 31, 2016, the pastor felt led to abandon the message he had prepared and instead referred to numerous scripture verses on healing. He said since God never changes, we should believe that

He will still heal His people! The pastor decided to step out in faith and asked for anyone dealing with on-going pain to come up to the front of the church. Since I had been dealing with chronic back pain for almost seven years, I went up to the front, along with many others. People gathered all around. The pastor prayed for everyone at the altar, asking that God might heal our bodies the way He had done so many times in the Bible. The music played. Folks were praying. It was incredible. I could feel the Holy Spirit moving. My friend put her hands on my lower back and began praying over me, asking God to heal me. I was sobbing and praying and begging God to heal me, even though it's something I had never really believed was possible. Suddenly, I felt a warmth and an "electricity" in my back and had a vision of myself running. When I stood up, I had no pain. When I walked to my seat, I had no pain. When I sat down in the chair, I had no pain!

Since my injury in 2009, I had endured test after test, had numerous injections, underwent spinal fusion surgery, endured countless hours of physical therapy, took several different medications every day, and lived with constant pain that no-one could explain. I was told that I would never run or ride a bike again. I was also told I could never sit on the floor or walk backwards. I spent more nights than I can count on the couch because of my back pain. It was extremely hard, but God brought so much good from it! I was able to be home with my children and homeschool them because of this injury. We were also able to purchase our home because of the worker's comp settlement. I had grown so much in my walk with Jesus through the experience as well! I had never really prayed for God to heal my back because I knew He was using it for good in my life. I guess I just assumed since God did this for me and my family, I just needed to deal with the pain as though it was my lot in life. Sadly, I never even considered asking God to heal my back. A week before the incredible healing service, Evan, who was four at the time, asked me why I had never asked God to heal my back. I didn't have a good answer, which caused me to start really pondering that question. The very next Sunday, I had the opportunity to be prayed over and healed! Even though I wanted to believe I was fully healed, I wondered if the pain would return. But it never did!

In May of 2016, when Tyson was about eight months old, another incredible thing occurred at the church we now called home. During a Sunday morning service, one of our pastors shared a message about going further with God. He said that we often want to go further in our walk with God, but we feel as though we can't. He explained it often happens because we have built up walls around our hearts that prevent us from growing deeper. We are selective with how we allow God to work in our lives. Additionally, we keep one or two things hidden in a corner of our hearts, build a wall around it, and are unwilling to release those things so that God can bring healing to our hearts. We can't go "all in" with God and be used by Him to the greatest extent, if we don't trust Him with all the areas of our lives, including our past. I felt as though the pastor was shining a spotlight on me. I knew, without doubt, this message was for me. My abortion had been one of those hidden issues in my heart for seventeen years. I had done a post-abortive Bible study and found some healing, but I had not experienced freedom. I had built up huge walls around my heart and had not allowed God to touch those places. I had been walking through life all that time completely covered in shame. I knew God was using this message to tell me, "It's time to stop hiding. It's time to step out of this secret and allow Me to heal your heart."

As soon as the service ended, I looked at Bryan and said, "I have to go talk with the pastor about the abortion." He understood and walked up to the front of the church with me. For the first time, I willingly shared my story, with someone other than Bryan or Melissa. The pastor was filled with compassion and shared many words of encouragement with me. He said, "Tori, sometimes the best way to break the walls down is to be transparent about the issues we've been hiding. I don't know what that looks like, but I feel sure God is going to use your story to bless us others in a mighty way." As I left church that day, I knew what I had to do. God had given me the idea to begin my blog, "A Life of Gratitude," five years earlier. People from all over the world read my blog on a regular basis, so I knew that was the avenue I needed to use to share my story.

I decided to tell my best friend, Vanessa, before sharing the blog because I didn't want her to find out while reading it, just like a stranger would. Later that afternoon, we met at a local frozen yogurt shop and sat outside on a beautiful, windy afternoon. I shared my secret with her through tears and shame. I wasn't sure how she would react, but I was pleasantly surprised by her compassion and love toward me. She encouraged me to move forward with telling my story and even said that I had altered her view of post-abortive women. She had always had an idea of women that would abort a child but now she could see that the situations aren't always so black and white. Observing her response gave me the fuel I needed to go forward with sharing my story on my blog that night.

I began writing the blog once I put the kids to bed. As I was preparing to share it on social media, I was tempted to back out. I was terrified of the impact this might have on the opinion others had of me. But I looked to my Savior and I saw how far He had carried me over the past seventeen years, and I knew that He wanted to set me free from the walls this secret had built up around me. The way to freedom in this case was transparency. I knew the secret would be a shock to many people and possibly cause hard feelings from some but, I couldn't worry over that anymore. Not sharing my story at that point would have been much worse than sharing it.

On Sunday, May 15, 2016, I shared my big, dark, ugly secret on the internet for the entire world to see. I was expecting to feel judged and mocked and ridiculed for sharing my secret. I knew God wanted me to be transparent with my story, but I never imagined all that He would do with it in such a short time!

Within twenty-four hours of writing that blog, I had three people reach out to me with similar stories. Within a few days, one thousand three hundred people had read the blog and countless others had shared an encouraging word with me. I expected to feel belittled and uncomfortable, but instead, God quickly allowed me to feel loved and accepted. I got a taste of what it felt like to be free from all shame and embarrassment. I was positively overwhelmed by the response to my secret. Satan made me believe that I was the only person with such a deep, dark thing in my past. He caused me to believe that sharing my story would provoke people to judge and dislike me. *Boy, was he wrong! What should I have expected from the Father of All Lies?* God immediately used my story to comfort others and give them the courage to share their stories with me. He also changed my fear into excitement! Suddenly, instead of wanting to hide my past, I wanted others to know what God had done in my life, even though my past was so ugly.

I fully intended never to share my secret with anyone, but once I did, I was astonished by the freedom it brought. I felt like a boulder had been lifted off my chest and I could finally breathe. I felt like my eyes had been uncovered and I finally saw things clearly. I felt like the sun started to shine in a place that had been in utter darkness for seventeen years. I felt totally released of all shame and guilt and fear. I realized, that the walls I had built around my heart to protect it, only served as a cage that caused more pain and held me down. But, truthfully, that cage had been open all along, I just needed to find the courage to step out of it. I began to fully understand that there is nothing like the freedom that is found in Christ!

23

A Daughter Completes the Family

I CONTINUED TO BE amazed by the freedom I was experiencing as the weeks went by. I had walked closely with Jesus for years and years but for some reason, I never believed that sharing my secret would do anything but hurt me. Following God in obedience and sharing so openly gave me a new, deeper friendship with Him that I never knew I could have. I was like a child running through an open field with my arms up in the air and the wind dancing through my hair.

I spoke often with many other post-abortive women through email and text, offering them hope and encouragement. I also had hopes of sharing my story with teenagers at our youth group, but that never seemed to work out. My church created a video of Bryan and I, discussing the abortion. The plan was to share the video with our church family at some point. Time went by though, and the video was never shared. I figured it just wasn't the right time and sort of let go of the idea to share my story in a broader sense.

In the months to follow, I was given the opportunity to be on the Board of Directors of the local pregnancy care center. I had supported this ministry in other ways in the past, by volunteering to sort through clothes and participate in their Walk for Life. Dylan and I had also created "Dylan's Diaper Doozie" in 2012 when the center was in desperate need of diapers and wipes. He raised over $1,000 for diapers and wipes and was even on the news! This had also been the place where I had silently planted flowers in honor of the baby I aborted. Vanessa became a Board Member for the pregnancy center, too. I considered it a great blessing to be a part of a life-giving ministry, especially alongside my friend.

In the summer of 2016, Vanessa had a miscarriage. It was a sad time for her and her family. My heart broke as I remembered how hard my miscarriage had been. Her family planned a balloon release in honor of their child, and they invited me to release balloons for my preborn babies as well. As I stood on a grassy hill and peered out across the lake, I released balloons in honor of my precious babies.

After seventeen years of pretending my first baby didn't exist, honoring that child and the baby I miscarried when I was twenty-five, was incredibly meaningful for me. I didn't expect all the emotions I felt and the many tears that fell, but I knew this experience was part of the healing that God had for me. As I processed the experience that evening, I felt the need to speak directly to my babies, as I had never really done before. And so, I wrote this short letter to the little ones I never adequately acknowledged.

> *To My Babies in Heaven . . .*
> *I released a balloon today for each of you.*
> *While I know they won't make it all the way to Heaven,*
> *I pray that God will let the love attached to them*
> *float up through the clouds to meet the two of you.*
> *While you're running around on the streets of gold,*
> *I hope you feel your mother's love surrounding you.*
> *Please know that you have each made*
> *an enormous impact on my heart and my life.*
> *I wish I could hold you and see your smiling faces,*
> *and one day, because of God's grace, I will.*
> *Until then, enjoy the beautiful days spent with Jesus*
> *and know that there isn't a day that goes by*
> *that I don't think of you both.*
> *-Mommy*

Healing continued to come here and there as I walked with God. Refusing to let shame cover me and confronting the feelings that popped up from time to time, helped me to grow and heal in many ways. Later that summer, Bryan and I, along with our kids, went to the pregnancy center with my friend and her family. We placed personalized bricks into their memorial garden, in honor of our preborn children. Having my family there with me was very special. Thankfully, this experience brought some closure to this area of my past.

In October 2016, just couple of months later, we discovered we were being blessed with baby number four! Our three little boys couldn't have been more thrilled! With every day that passed, they showed concern for how sick I was, asked questions about the baby's development, and put their arms around my growing belly. I felt different during this pregnancy than I had with all the others. I still dealt with the same physical symptoms, but there was a beautiful peace I hadn't experienced with my other pregnancies. Knowing that I wasn't hiding the terrible secret of my first pregnancy, allowed me to rest and enjoy this pregnancy in a much broader way.

Vanessa found out she was pregnant too, about two weeks after me. We both had three little boys of similar ages and we both homeschooled. We journeyed through our pregnancies together and prayed that God would allow us both to have daughters.

When I was about twelve weeks pregnant, I decided to have DNA testing done. We never had it done with our previous pregnancies because the results wouldn't have changed our love for our child but, this time, I wanted actual testing done to determine the sex of our child. The surprise during our last delivery wasn't something I wanted to experience again! We waited with excitement for a couple of weeks for the results to come in. On December 1st, while driving alone in my car, I received a phone call from my doctor's office. The nurse said, "Congratulations, your daughter is completely healthy!" This moment was beautiful in so many ways. Most parents with three sons would be thrilled with the news of having a daughter, but this was extra special because of the shocking birth of our third son, after being told he was a girl. I also knew that God had allowed me to be alone when I heard the news because of all those nights alone, when I had called out to Him. During those nights, I asked Him a lot of hard questions and He assured me His plans were good and He was doing all of this for me. As I sat in the car, pondering the gift of three boys and now a baby girl, I realized how precious the timing of *this* daughter was. I was a different person now. Surrendering my secret several months prior had opened parts of me that I hadn't known existed. God spoke to me, in that moment, and I knew that my first pregnancy had also been a daughter. I needed these precious boys to comfort my heart through the years of finding healing from my abortion-*and boy, had they ever!* Now, was the perfect time for my second daughter to be born.

When I returned home that day, Bryan and I gave the boys cans of silly string and "went live" on Facebook to share the good news! The boys were over-the-top excited when pink string sprayed out of the can! We were a little shocked, but with a DNA test we could be almost certain it really was a girl! Our families and friends were excited for us too. Another sweet friend, who also had three boys, "bombed" our house that afternoon with tons of pink streamers, balloons, and confetti. It was such a fun surprise and something I'll never forget. There was celebration all around because of this exciting news. In my heart I knew, the celebration appeared to be about the child's gender, but in reality, it was God's way of showering more and more love on me. He was reiterating his desire for this pregnancy to be different than my others because of the freedom I had finally accepted from him.

At the end of May 2017, our sweet Allison entered the world. Throughout my pregnancy, I spent time asking God who this baby would be. One of the words I heard over and over was, "joy-bringer." *I know that isn't a real word but there couldn't have been a better description for this precious girl.* From the moment she was born, I knew God's words to me about her were true.

Our last addition, Allison, our "joy-bringer"

Believe it or not, my friend Vanessa ended up having an emergency c-section the very same day I gave birth to Allison. She also had a baby girl. Within a few days of their births, the daughters we had prayed for and carried together over the past nine months, met for the first time. God had been so present in the details of our pregnancies and in the births of these girls we had asked Him for.

Watching Bryan with his new daughter and my sons with their sister, was an incredibly sweet time for me. I felt like a different person; like someone who was finally free to truly enjoy the gifts God had given her. I'm not sure there has ever been a little girl more loved by her brothers, or her daddy. She immediately brought so much joy into our home.

There was no question that God's plan for our family was perfect. We had never dreamed of having four children. Truthfully, a tubal ligation was scheduled for just hours after our third child was born. But after the shock we experienced, we decided to wait on that procedure. It wasn't because we were unhappy with a boy being born, we just couldn't make such a final decision with the make-up of our family being altered so abruptly. The decision to wait on having my tubes tied after baby number three, resulted in another pregnancy two and a half years later. Even though the thought of having four kids was overwhelming and seemed absurd to so many in our generation, we were thrilled that God would allow us to have another child. We honestly would have been 100% happy with another son, too. But God knew all along that our fourth child would be a baby girl and that I wouldn't be the mother she needed until I had experienced true healing several months before she was born. So much had changed in my heart since sharing my story openly. I felt free from shame and guilt. I cared less and less about the opinion of others. I finally saw value in myself and began learning how to silence the lies I had been listening to for so long. I was ready to be a role model for a young lady; to teach her to find her identity in her Savior, and to help her understand how valuable and loved she truly is.

24

Rejected Again

I EXPERIENCED POSTPARTUM DEPRESSION after all three of my sons were born so I wasn't too surprised when the all too familiar symptoms began to arise. But a few different symptoms popped up after Allison's birth too, ones that concerned me a great deal. Stiffness over my entire body in the mornings that took over an hour to fade, severe fatigue, unexplained weight gain, muscle pain throughout my body, "brain fog," and extreme discomfort around my ribcage, just to name a few. I went to doctor after doctor and continued to be brushed off. They would treat one symptom or even blame all my issues on being a mom. "Mothers are tired," they would say, or "once your baby is sleeping through the night, you'll feel better." I began to wonder if I was crazy. *Were all these symptoms normal? Surely not.* I could barely walk in the mornings and couldn't hold my eyes open in the afternoons. Most moms weren't feeling this way. Friends and family pushed products, oils, exercise programs, and quick fixes on me, each believing their idea would completely cure me. I tried everything I could to feel better, but nothing seemed to work.

Life goes on though, even if you're not feeling well. Being a home-schooling mom with four children was busy but fun. I spent a lot of time with my friend Vanessa, whose baby was born the same day as Allison. We worked diligently to plan two big events for the pregnancy care center and enjoyed letting our kids play together. After one of the events we planned and executed for the center, something happened between the two of us. I'm honestly completely unsure what it was. That December, when our babies were six months old, she decided not to talk to me any longer. Without explaining the reasons behind her choice, she blocked me out of her life as though I was suddenly her enemy.

We had been very close friends. We had spent a lot of time together and had so much in common. We both had three boys and were home-school moms. We had been pregnant with our daughters at the same and they had even been born on the same day. We had spent hours and hours working on projects for the pregnancy care center. We both desired to grow in our faith, and we spurred each other on in that way. We walked alongside one another and encouraged one another through some very difficult things. Our kids had become best friends too, through hours of play dates and field trips.

I had such a hard time wrapping my mind around her decision to discard my family. I had so many questions and she refused to answer even one. The pain of rejection and abandonment I had known so well in my childhood, college years, and with my parents a few years prior, forced its way back into my heart. This situation left me feeling like garbage; completely worthless and thrown away. It was compounded by the ache in the hearts of my children. They asked repeatedly when they could see their friends. They began to think their friends didn't like them anymore or they must have done something wrong. It was my desire to hide the truth of the situation from them because I didn't want to say anything negative about Vanessa, but after a while, it became clear things weren't going to change. So, I gently explained to my boys that they wouldn't be able to see their friends anymore because their mom didn't want to see me. It was a terribly difficult conversation because I couldn't answer any of the questions they had.

Although the loss of such a close friend was something I wish had never happened, God taught me many things through it. For months, I struggled with feeling forgotten and easily replaced, but God began to show me that He had not forgotten me. Even when others "threw me away," I was overwhelmed with His blessings. I had four beautiful children that constantly reminded me of my value and helped me feel loved. I had a husband that spoke truth over me, reminding that I am irreplaceable. I had a church family that encouraged my spiritual growth and showed great concern for me. My biological family had been restored in remarkable ways. I had been forgiven and set free from a life of shame and guilt. I had been allowed to speak life into other women who were currently trying to find that same freedom. I had the gift of spending every day with my family, homeschooling my children, and protecting them from worldly influences. I had a

Heavenly Father that would always stay, no matter what. These blessings and God's promise to never leave or forsake me, carried me through another season of rejection. Having these gifts in my life allowed me to come out on the other side of this painful time, with a new dependency on the only One who would never leave me. I realized the beauty of believing what my Heavenly Father says about me, whether the people in my life agree with Him or not. I believed that He could be trusted even in the situations that made no sense and hurt the most.

25

Built for this Battle

I CONTINUED TO DEAL with all my physical issues, however, the rejection served as a distraction for a while. I hadn't felt like myself in many years. I struggled for hours every morning with full body muscle stiffness coupled with excruciating neck pain and draining fatigue. I had visited so many doctors over the years and none had ever been able to figure out what caused me to feel so bad. I was misdiagnosed and prescribed all sorts of medicines. I was given supplements and exercises to try. I tried integrative specialists, and countless different diets, and at least four of those all-natural programs that guarantee to help all that ails you. I did everything I could to fix what was wrong with me, to no avail.

In 2018 my symptoms worsened; I began having severe pain on the left side of my body. It started in my foot, then the knuckles on my left hand started to swell and hurt terribly. Next my entire left leg began to hurt, so badly sometimes that I couldn't walk. I began having a lot of pain in my chest and ribcage, too. I remember one day specifically; I was taking the boys to summer camp and I suddenly wasn't sure if I could make it from the church door back to my car. That was the day I knew something had to be done.

I decided to try an urgent care. Unlike so many of the doctors I had seen, the urgent care doctor was thorough and compassionate and believed that something much more complicated was going on. He did several blood tests that proved his theory and said I needed to see a rheumatologist right away.

At my first rheumatology appointment, forty-two tests were performed in order to find out what was going on with me. After two weeks and three days, my new doctor called with my diagnosis. This diagnosis was different than the things she had mentioned previously, therefore it was not at all what I was expecting to hear. She told me the test proved that I had Ankylosing Spondylitis.

I had never heard of it before, but quickly researched and discovered that Ankylosing Spondylitis is a rare auto-immune disease. Most typically the spine is the focal point of the disease, but it also affects the ribcage, hips, feet, hands, and other peripheral joints. As with all auto-immune disorders, the immune system is attacking the healthy parts of the body. The difference with AS is that the body will try to heal itself by growing new bone in the spine and other joints. This can lead to spinal fusion and cause the spine to curve permanently. Chronic fatigue, extreme muscle stiffness, pain and difficulty when breathing, eye problems, muscle soreness, and flare-ups on one side of the body, also play a major role in AS.

The day I received that diagnosis was difficult. I spent hours picturing myself as the Hunchback of Notre Dame, angry because this isn't a disease that anyone understands or even knows about, and fearing what my future might look like. *Will I become deformed? Will I lose mobility in my spine, hips, hands, feet? Will I lose my eyesight? Will my breathing become impaired because my ribs calcify? Will there ever be relief from this pain I'm dealing with?* Ankylosing Spondylitis is not life-threatening but let's be honest, it definitely threatened the quality of my life.

During the previous weeks, as I awaited the test results, I had been praying and deciding to believe that God knew exactly what He is doing, no matter what. That truth didn't change with this shocking diagnosis. The enemy was using this to instill fear within me. So, I called out to God in desperation, and right then, He spoke to my heart. As I prayed, God said, "Tori, you don't need to be overwhelmed. I built you for this battle." And like an epiphany I realized, He knew before I was born what I difficulties I would face, and with his help, I would have all I needed to be victorious.

I decided to believe, if this was the road I must travel, God would be with me every step of the way. He had been preparing my heart for this. I was reminded that He is in control, He is my source of strength, and He has purpose for everything I endure.

I was also incredibly grateful for a diagnosis. After so many years of feeling like no one believed me and searching for answers without finding any; finally knowing what I was dealing with was truly a blessing. My previous health concerns and the difficulty I had healing from surgeries made perfect sense with this diagnosis. I didn't want to have AS, but there was power in finally knowing what I was fighting. After all, I was ready to fight because God built me for this battle.

I designed this shirt to wear to my first infusion therapy appointment

The months that followed were tough. I started several new medications; some of which caused a nasty allergic reaction. I began taking chemotherapy pills every Wednesday night and was forced to lay on the couch or in the bed for the next three days. I was dealing with all my usual symptoms, but they were all compounded because of these medications. My doctor assured me it always took time to find the right "cocktail" of medications, and in time, we found a good combination. It took over six months for my insurance company to approve the infusion therapy that would have the greatest impact on my pain and my prognosis. In January of 2019, I began receiving infusion therapy every seven to eight weeks. After the initial loading doses of this biologic drug, I was filled with so much hope. I finally felt a little like myself again.

26

An Unlikely Place to Encounter
a Redeeming God

ALMOST THREE YEARS AFTER sharing my big scary secret with the world, the pastor at my church asked if I would be willing to create a video, sharing my story and the freedom in Christ I had found. I knew immediately that God had provided this opportunity as another level of healing for me. Now that I was on the right track with the treatment for Ankylosing Spondylitis and feeling somewhat better, I agreed to create the video.

In March 2019, the story of my abortion, the shame and guilt that followed, and the forgiveness I had found, was shared during a Sunday morning church service. Watching myself say the ugly truth out loud was surreal. I cringed and gripped Bryan's hand. As the video came to an end, I awaited accusatory stares from everyone in the room. Instead, the pastor asked Bryan and me to stand up, and as we did, everyone began to clap for us. Soon, everyone in the room was standing in appreciation of my willingness to share something that's typically hidden.

Within days the video had been viewed over four-thousand times online. Those days were filled with conversations. Some people thanked me for my courage. Others said they were sorry for what I had been through. A few even said I had changed their view of post-abortive women. But mostly, those conversations were with other post-abortive women who finally felt the freedom to share their secret with someone; someone they knew wouldn't judge them. My heart was broken for these women because

I knew exactly what they were feeling. I prayed for them often and felt led to begin a post-abortive Bible study at my church.

There were originally eight women who had signed up for the post-abortive study, but we ended up with a group four. Even though the study was held on a weeknight, and they were able to use a discreet entrance, several of the ladies just couldn't bring themselves to come to church. They were afraid someone would see them enter the building and associate them with the post abortive group. I understood that feeling of shame very well.

A week after my video was shared, our church family attended a pre-premiere of a movie telling the story of a former abortion facility manager. I walked into that movie theater feeling confident in my decision to be transparent about my abortion, but I walked out completely covered in shame, again. I wanted to hide my face as I walked through the lobby. I felt as if everyone there was staring at me. The movie had not sugarcoated abortion at all. So, after watching it, everyone knew exactly what I had done. It was as if I picked up the chains that had bound me for so long and tightened them around my wrists once again.

All night and the next morning, I wrestled with guilt, shame, fear, and worthlessness. I spent some time in my prayer closet and heard God say, "You have to face this head on." As ridiculous as it seemed, I knew I had to go back to the beginning, back to the clinic I had visited almost twenty years before. I had never returned and had tried so hard to forget that terrible place. I didn't even know where it was. I looked online for information and discovered the clinic had been closed for many years. I couldn't find the exact address, so I sent my mom a text, asking if she remembered. I was shocked to receive a text back with the address for the clinic. Even though we had only been there together one time and it was in a town we didn't live in, after almost twenty years, my mom remembered the address. *I guess that awful time in our lives affected her more than I realized.*

After working up the courage, I drove to the address she had given me and parked in the parking lot. There were two buildings that looked very similar sitting right next to each other. I decided to enter one and ask what business used to be in the building, just so I could know which one was truly the former clinic. As I walked up the little sidewalk to the front entrance, my heart raced, and my palms became sweaty. I knew, before even asking, that this was the place. I walked through the heavy, green door and felt as if the wind was knocked out of me. There was a heaviness that couldn't be explained. I struggled to contain my tears. A young lady stood behind a counter and I asked her timidly, "Do you know what business was here before yours?" She looked at me oddly and said in a whisper, "I've been told it was an abortion clinic." I felt the color drain from my cheeks. She had confirmed what I already knew but hearing her say the words had an effect on me. I was standing in the place where my baby was aborted.

I said thank you as fast as I could and nearly tripped over a rug as I rushed out the door and back to my car. I jumped inside and slammed the door, as if it could protect me from something lurking outside. I sat there, for a while, in a daze. Looking at those mismatched bricks was crushing. I could barely contain the emotions that were rising within me. I gave myself permission to journey through the memories of the first time I had been there, which is something I had never really done. I envisioned myself walking through the green door, through the small lobby area, and then into the waiting room. Memories I had attempted to discard and worked so hard to forget, began to surface. I saw myself walking through the halls, entering a dim room, and going through the most traumatic thing I had ever experienced. Memories of the recovery room and the nurses came flooding back as well. It was all too much. Tears poured down my cheeks, and at times, I felt as if I couldn't catch my breath. Through my tears, I prayed, and God comforted my heart.

Captured outside the former abortion clinic the first time I revisited it

I played worship music, read scripture, and thought about the child whose life I ended. I named her Taylor several years prior, but suddenly I needed to know the meaning behind the name. Using my cell phone, I looked up the meaning of my daughter's name. What I found touched my soul in a beautiful way.

Taylor = clothed with salvation; eternal beauty.

I wrote in my journal, just trying to get out all the thoughts that were swirling in my head. I spent so many years bottling things up, I was determined not to do that again.

> "*Sitting outside of the place where I had an abortion.*
> *This is where my baby died, along with so many others.*
> *This is where I've refused to come and where I've refused to go in my mind.*
> *This is where the enemy took something from me and thought he would forever hold it over my head.*
> *This is where my freedom was ripped away.*
> *This is where my nightmares began, the hate for myself began, and the belief that I have no value was solidified.*
> *This is where my story changed and where I began to turn away from Jesus.*
> *This is where I sit and mourn my baby, my choice, my secret life, my fear, my shame, and my past.*
> *But I know there is a power that can break shackles, even the ones bound, locked, and worn for over half of one's life.*
> *Twenty years. Two decades since I willingly let someone rip my child from my womb.*
> *Right here, in this very place.*
> *I wish I could go back to that day, to that girl who entered the building one way but when she left, she would never be the same.*
> *I wish I could tell her that abortion isn't the right choice.*
> *I wish I could hug her and help her understand what she was about to do.*
> *But it wouldn't matter. What's done is done.*
> *If I could go back and change my mind; would I really want to?*
> *This is part of my story.*
> *This is something God will use in a HUGE way.*
> *This helped to make me who I am – God's masterpiece.*
> *This building contains the memories of thousands of murdered babies.*
> *My baby had a purpose.*
> *And part of that purpose was that one day I would sit here, twenty years later, and grieve the loss, share my heartache with God, and remember all that God has done since then.*
> *To allow my memory to open and no longer hide my child.*
> *To allow light in on this darkness, and to be encouraged to push forward, unashamed and willing, to let God use Taylor's story however He'd like.*"

I was able to calm down, and asked God to speak to me about this wretched thing from my past. My journal was still laying on my lap, along with a pen. As soon as I began to hear His voice, I started scribbling down everything He said as fast as I could. It's so hard to explain but it seemed as if His voice boomed from within me, but in the gentlest way.

He said,

"Your baby is ok, Tori.
She is here with Me.
She is proud of you.
She is not mad at you.
She loves the plans I have for you.
She wants you to share the story of her life.
All of this has a purpose.
Your emotions are reminding you why this is so important.
You are my faithful daughter and I trust you with this story.
You will help change this nightmare and keep others from feeling this pain.
This building once was a place of evil, but it no longer is.
I ended that clinic.
No more lives are taken here.
No more.
Your body was once a place of shame. It no longer is.
I ended the hold the enemy had on you.
No more shame covers you.
No more.
I make all things new.
Now go, allow me use your story and strengthen you."

His words comforted my heart in a way that cannot be explained. My tears changed from desperate cries to joy overflowing from within me. *Who would have ever guessed? My most intimate encounter with my Heavenly Father would be in the last place I ever wanted to go.*

I had lost a piece of me, right there, in that ugly brick building, and God lead me precisely where I needed to go to find it.

I didn't know exactly what He had in store for my future, but the fear and shame that engulfed me as I drove into that parking lot, were eradicated by a holy, mighty God. I knew He had big plans and I knew I had to follow Him. I drove away from the former clinic with the thought, *"The enemy repeatedly tries to bury me. Funny thing is, he doesn't know I am a seed."*

27

The Year of Big Things

I DIDN'T KNOW IT at the time, but things would never be the same after revisiting the former clinic. The following month I began advocating for life on the sidewalk outside of two different abortion clinics in my area. I met many other pro-life advocates and began to realize I had been surprisingly ignorant about the issue of abortion. I attended prayer walks, watched documentaries, read article after article, and soaked up as much information as I could. It was apparent that God wanted me to take a stand on this issue. *But how?*

The Lord began to lay ideas on my heart and fill me with a compassion I hadn't experienced before. I desired for Him to use my story to help save the lives of babies, but also save the lives of women who would never be the same after making the choice to abort their child. I began having snippets of a vision. God was revealing His plan bit by bit. *If He had revealed it all at once, it would have probably overwhelmed me and caused fear to rise within me.*

One day, as I stood outside a clinic, I talked with two, more experienced, pro-life advocates. I shared my desire to help create a more consistent sidewalk presence at the clinic in the same town where I had my abortion. As we talked, one of the men explained that a building beside the clinic in that town was for lease. He continued to talk but I didn't hear any more of his words. My mind was whirling. It was like puzzle pieces coming together in my mind. The picture still wasn't clear, but I was beginning to see what God had in store.

Later that week, I was flooded with ideas and thoughts that I jotted down in the same journal I had scribbled in while sitting in front of the former clinic. The ministry God had for me was called, "Not Forgotten Ministries." It would be near the active abortion clinic in the same town where I aborted my child. It would be a comfortable reprieve, welcoming and full of love, a place of light and hope. This is where post-abortive Bible studies would be held, and where sidewalk counselors would be trained. I also had a clear vision of our memorial for the preborn. It would be called "Taylor's Tribute" in honor of my baby.

I was filled with excitement and a boldness I had never experienced before. After discussing things with Bryan, I quit my side job with a direct sales company and chose to believe God would provide for my family. I arranged childcare for my children two mornings a week and set out on the mission God had given me.

I met with my pastors who encouraged me to follow God, without worrying over the money needed to do so. They inspired me to move forward and begin searching for a location close to the clinic. I quickly realized there were several places surrounding the clinic for sale or rent. I called each one, made appointments to visit many of them, and got shut down by all of them. Each property manager would say something like, "We agree with what you're doing, but we want to stay out of it." The owner of a little building, right behind the clinic, said, "I want nothing to do with you, or your ministry." For a few weeks, the property directly across the street from the clinic was onboard with my mission. There was even a lease drawn up. The owner went on vacation and when he returned, the realtor informed me he had changed his mind and no longer wanted to rent the space to a ministry like mine. The enemy didn't like what I was doing, and he did everything he could to try and stop me. God reminded me that the pro-life movement is scary to most people. He told me I was like Elisha, from Second Kings 4:32–35. I was laying and breathing on my community, trying to awaken people who had been spiritually dead. When my first, second, and third attempts didn't work, I kept on going.

During the same time period, I was struggling personally, in a very challenging way. While Bryan was supportive of my desire to help women choose life and find healing from past abortions, he was not fully on board with this vision God had given me. He wanted me to follow God, but he was concerned with the way I was doing it. I am a "full steam ahead" sort of person. When I set my mind to something, I do it. When I have big ideas, I'm not afraid to go after them and sometimes, I don't think about things from all angles. Bryan, on the other hand, is cautious and reserved, which has been good in most situations and a great compliment to me as well. The problem is, in this case at least, stepping lightly and moving carefully wasn't what God was asking of me. Bryan's concerns were numerous, and he wasn't afraid to point them out. I began to feel as if he was my biggest obstacle. This situation shed light on resentment in my heart toward my husband that had gone unresolved. *He left me to deal with the abortion by myself. He made me carry the burden alone for all those years. And he's making me do this alone as well!* It was terribly hard for me to move forward with my calling while feeling as if Bryan was fighting against it and our marriage was suffering because of it. I was losing the confidence God had given me to move forward and I began to question everything I was so sure I had heard. I spent hours in my prayer closet, asking God to have His way. He revealed that faith is God-sized confidence, so I didn't really need any confidence of my own. I just need to have faith in Him.

In May I was asked to be a mentor for a young lady in my area who had chosen life outside of an abortion clinic. I was honored to do so but felt inadequate and unprepared. We had many conversations that began with her considering going back to the clinic but ended with her reaffirming her choice to keep her baby. The opportunity to use my experience to help a young mother make a different choice, solidified my desire to be an active participant in the pro-life movement.

Around this time, I also had a strong desire to learn more about my abortion experience. During the procedure in 1999, I was not allowed to know how far along I was or see the ultrasound, but now, I needed to know something, anything to connect me more with those memories. I didn't remember the date of the procedure and neither did my mom. I only knew the year because of it happening right before Bryan left for college. I searched and searched online, but nothing could be found from that clinic. Because my abortion happened so long ago, I doubted I would find any relevant information. One day my mom suggested I call the hospital where I had spent the night prior to the abortion. She previously worked in the medical records department at that hospital and knew they kept medical records as far back as 1960. I called immediately. The lady I spoke with said they may have the actual record stored in a vault, but it would take several weeks to find. Once they found my record, they would mail it to me. However, she could see the dates of hospital stays in her computer system. So, by the end of the phone call, I knew the date of my night in the hospital.

It was June 18, 1999.

The Year of Big Things

So that means my baby was aborted on June 19, 1999. I walked out of that horrific place covered in shame on June 19, 1999. My life forever changed on June 19, 1999.

Knowing the date of my abortion empowered me. It shed more light on the darkness that haunted my past. I may not know the specifics about my baby, but I did know the day she was welcomed into heaven, and that information was priceless. I decided that I would return to the clinic and go inside on the twentieth anniversary. Throughout the past few months, I had met several other post-abortive women. I asked one precious lady, who had become a friend, if she would go back to the clinic with me. She agreed and was a much-needed support system as I entered the building again and asked to talk with the owner.

I didn't know what to expect. *Maybe these people would think I was crazy? Maybe they would laugh at me or ridicule me, or even kick me out?* We waited on the owner to come out to speak with us but instead, an employee ushered us back to her office. I put one foot in front of the other and made my way through those eerie hallways. It was surreal. We sat down in her office and I shared my story with her. I was waiting to hear a condemning voice or see a confused expression but instead, she gently said, "I am so proud of you." She explained that when she purchased the building, she knew it had once been an abortion clinic. Her family had prayed over the building and she had asked God to heal the women who once stepped foot there. *God really had done a new thing in this place!*

She gave us a tour through the building, pointing out the rooms and what they had been used for in years past. She showed us the waiting areas and the recovery room. She pointed out the dispensary, where the contents of the jars were placed on a baking dish with a light underneath and pieced back together to ensure no body parts had been left inside the mother's uterus. She showed us the back door where the bags of remains were tossed into the bio-hazard waste bins. And then, she led me to the rooms where the procedures were performed. The wind was knocked out of me as I stepped inside a room that now served as an employee lounge. *This was it. This was where my baby died.* Memories flooded my mind and tears trickled down my face. But as quickly as the sadness came, it left, and an overwhelming peace took its place.

My motive in going back inside the clinic can be traced back to the story of the Israelites in the book of Joshua. After wandering for forty years in the desert, they were finally about to enter the Promised Land. God parted the Jordan River for them to pass through (just as he had parted the Red Sea for their ancestors) and told them to gather twelve stones from the river to be placed in a circle as a memorial, a reminder for future generations of God's great faithfulness. This was done at Gilgal which means, "circle of stones" and represents coming full circle.

It had been my desire, and the owner of the building encouraged me, to create a memorial for Taylor somewhere on the property. So, I was able to mark *my* Gilgal right outside the back door of the clinic, where my baby would have been tossed into the bin. It took twenty years, but God brought me full circle. Using stones with scriptures, my baby's name, and the date of my abortion written on them, I created a memorial of God's faithfulness for myself and for anyone else that might need the reminder.

That experience brought more healing to my heart and was like fuel to my fire. If God could take my brokenness and make it into something beautiful, I was going to let Him! But of course, the enemy tried to stop me every chance he could. I began having terrible eye issues, which is something I had never experienced before. First, I had a scratched cornea, then a few weeks later I broke my eye. The sclera, or the white part of the eye had cracked open. After a few more weeks, I began experiencing Recurrent Corneal Erosions, which means the outer layer of the cornea continuously stuck to my eyelid and was peeled off in the mornings. All these eye issues were incredibly painful and forced me to keep my eyes shut for days at a time. The enemy hated that I was opening the eyes of so many to the truth of abortion, so he was trying to hinder my sight.

Everywhere I turned, I found references to the story of Esther in the Bible. It became obvious I needed to learn more about the story. Even though it seemed impossible, Esther was able to use her position as Queen to rescue her people from destruction. As I studied, God spoke to my heart. *This* was my Esther moment. He had positioned me, just as He had positioned Esther, for such a time as this. All I needed was His favor, which would open doors no one could close. The rocky road I've traveled allowed me to understand the importance of this calling. And now this moment would cause me to see that the wilderness was worth it.

Through the summer, I searched for properties near the clinic, began leading sidewalk advocacy trainings, initiated the process of raising funds, continued leading post-abortive studies, began leading mentor trainings, and submitted all the paperwork to incorporate Not Forgotten Ministries and to become an official 501c3 nonprofit ministry. In July, I hosted Not

Forgotten Ministries' very first board meeting in my dining room. It was incredible to see seven other people who believed in the mission God had given me. One of which was Dee, who had visited me in the hospital the evening before my abortion. She just happened to be visiting someone else when she saw my mom in the hallway. It was a quick visit that didn't mean much at the time, but now, twenty years later, her support and involvement served as another affirmation from God, that I have truly come full circle.

On July 12th I came across a small space, only a block away from the clinic, with a huge sign that read, "for lease." The realtor I had been working with called the number provided but never received a call back. When I called on July 14th, I got a return call within an hour. I saw the space and immediately knew it was the spot God had for the ministry. The landlord needed the lease to be signed by July 17th. So, I had three days to raise $2,800.00. The Board voted to sign the lease if the funds were raised in time. It seemed like a long shot, but God came through and I signed the lease on July 17th. Within four days, the entire office was completely furnished with donated items. Not only were the items in good condition or brand new, they all matched the ministry's color-scheme I had designed a few months before. This may have seemed trivial to some, but I knew it was another way God was reassuring me that I was on the right path. Even though the color scheme didn't really matter, it did matter to me. I wanted the building to be a beautiful, welcoming, peaceful reprieve, and that is exactly what God had allowed me to create as the donated items were brought in, piece by piece.

Not Forgotten Ministries Headquarters

Even though it was apparent God was at work through the ministry and was providing everything I needed, Bryan was still stingy with his support. From the outside, it appeared we were a team, but on the inside, I had never felt more alone. I was hurting deeply because I felt torn between God's calling and my husband's approval. But more so, this experience was drudging up handfuls of bitterness with very deep roots. *This isn't only my story. It's his story, too. I've carried it alone for twenty years. God is turning it into something beautiful, why can't he see that?*

Memorial Service for Victims of Abortion, September 2019

On August 4th Not Forgotten Ministries hosted an Open House and Dedication at our new location. Soon after, our advocacy team began having a consistent presence outside the abortion clinic, the first post-abortive Bible study on location began, and memorials were being created in honor of pre-born babies. In September, we hosted a beautiful memorial service for victims of abortion and in November we hosted a fundraising luncheon. God also orchestrated a partnership with a ministry in Pakistan which typically ministers to young children. Two pregnant women in their community had decided to abort their children and since the ministry had no experience in this area, they sought out help. By God's design, they found Not Forgotten Ministries through Facebook and reached out to me. I was able to create a video explaining the stages of development in the womb and another exposing the truth about abortion using photos and diagrams that would help them clearly understand what abortion would do to their preborn child. The videos were translated for the women and they each chose life for their babies! The women were so grateful for my help, they both asked me to name their sons! I chose Biblical names that mean Beloved and God is gracious.

Somewhere, amid all the things God was doing with the ministry, He did something even greater than I could imagine. I don't know what changed or what spurred the sudden support, but out of nowhere, Bryan became my biggest fan. *All those hours praying in my closet were full of such purpose.* God answered this very personal prayer in a beautiful way. Bryan began coming with me to the office, helping me create videos, making sure I had the things I needed for the events I hosted, and showing real concern for the heartbreak I had endured alone for twenty years. God was using the ministry to help other women find healing, to save the lives of babies, and provide a place for preborn lives to be honored, but the thing that blessed my heart more than anything else was how He used it to heal our marriage, in ways only He could.

28

Stepping Back Inside the Nightmare

I DID SOMETHING I never imagined I could do.

A few years prior, the thought of telling someone my story made me sick to my stomach but now, God wanted me to share it openly and boldly. I was willing to step back into my nightmare because God had turned my brokenness into something beautiful. He changed everything for me. It wasn't something I did, other than just being willing. He provided forgiveness, healing, and freedom that I cannot describe.

In November, Angela Forker, of the "After the Abortion" photography series, flew from Indiana to North Carolina to tell my story through conceptual imagery. The photo shoot took place inside the former clinic where I had the abortion twenty years before. Being back inside that building, reliving that day, and allowing someone to see the full reality of my past, caused an overwhelming flood of emotions to come over me. There was also

a heaviness in and around the building that was inexplicable. I thought it was just a feeling I noticed because of my history inside those walls, but as soon as we drove in the parking lot, Angela felt it too. I can't adequately express the impact this photo session had on me. It was brutal, ugly, and powerful, all at the same time.

Angela did an amazing job depicting my memories and emotions

so that others could see the truth about abortion. It was eerie though, to see myself back inside the place I spent years trying to forget. The location of each photo taken was also symbolic.

The first photo was captured by the front door of the former abortion clinic. I entered believing I was making the right choice. I couldn't have been more wrong.

The second photo was taken in the former patient waiting room. Those drab walls were etched into my memory. I remember staring at those mismatched bricks, and crying, as I waited.

The third photo was taken by the side door where patients exited the building. The clinic employees knew it wasn't smart for anyone in the waiting to room to see the post-abortive women leaving. Angela instructed me to continue wearing the hospital gown for this photo and several others because it signified the shroud of shame and despair I invisibly wore for all those years. Though I became an expert at concealing it, it was with me constantly.

The fourth photo was taken inside the patient bathroom. What you can't see in this photo is the line of toilets against the wall without any doors. When we walked into this room, I had the most vivid memory that shook me to my core. This photo speaks the most to me, probably because I worked so hard to hide my secret for seventeen years.

The fifth photo was taken in the dispensary. I sat under the counter where the babies had been pieced back together to ensure nothing was left behind in their mother's womb. The room directly across the hall from the dispensary was where my procedure occurred. That room was where I began hiding. That was the room where the belief that my life had no value was solidified. That was the

room where I began wanting more than anything to pretend it had never happened. Angela was able to depict those feelings so well in this photo.

The sixth photo was taken right outside the back door of the former clinic. The employees exited through that door to toss the babies' remains in the bins. I placed the memorial to my sweet Taylor, right there on June 19, 2019, the twentieth anniversary of the abortion. It blessed my heart to find that the memorial was still there in November when we took the photos.

The final photo was my personal favorite. Bryan and I were standing on the very spot where discarded babies were tossed. Most post-abortive women aren't married to their baby's father but by God's grace, I am. The significance of this photo cannot be expressed. Together we stood in that spot, knowing our first child is safe in the arms of God. That was the first time we had been to that place together. Having the moment captured was such a gift to me.

Angela's God-given ability to portray the raw emotion that comes along with abortion, is giving post-abortive women the perfect vehicle to shed light on the topic of abortion. Her work with the "After the Abortion" photography series is breath-taking. Her time with me in the former clinic was incredible, and the photos are undeniably powerful. There were most likely some people who didn't understand why I would expose my secret in such a way and I'm sure others cringed at my transparency, but that was 100% okay with me because I knew God had plans to use my story to help other women who were suffering silently.

While reliving the experience of my abortion within the very walls where my nightmare began, I gained a new perspective. I began to realize that post-abortive women are the missing key to the pro-life movement.

If post-abortive women are bold enough to expose the truth about abortion and what it really does to women, we *can* change the opinion of our generation. Only those who have experienced this nightmare can adequately reveal abortion's true impact. However, in order for a post-abortive woman to feel comfortable sharing her story, it's imperative for pro-life advocates to lead with love, the way Jesus did. Abortion-minded and post-abortive women have been terrified to discuss the situations they face or the abortions in their past because of the judgement they feel from the church and the pro-life movement. Most pro-life advocates have good intentions and they desire to save the lives of preborn children. Though it is an admirable cause, often the way it's carried out provokes very vulnerable women to run faster inside the clinic. We need to keep it simple, love them, and let God change their minds and hearts. Without love, we will only push the women away. To save the lives of innocent, preborn children, we need to first reach the heart of their mothers. It's my prayer that God will use my story, the photos taken by Angela, and the ministry He has given me to alter the view so many people have of post-abortive women, to help those women find healing in Jesus, and to give them the courage to share their stories. Shedding light on the hidden, shadowy topic of abortion, will force the darkness to flee. There's no limit to the affect our honesty may have.

29

He's Not Finished Yet

IN DECEMBER, THE YOUNG mother I had been mentoring asked me to be present for the birth of her baby girl. I was filled with excitement and anticipation as I waited upon her arrival. When she was just a few hours old, I was able to hold the little miracle God had allowed me to help save. Joy filled my heart as she squeezed my finger and looked at me with her beautiful brown eyes.

By June 2020, a little more than a year after my story was shared via video with my church family and then on the internet for the world to see, Not Forgotten Ministries had helped save the lives of twenty-eight babies through sidewalk advocacy, mentoring, and our partnership in Pakistan. With our help, twenty-three post abortive women and one man began their journey toward healing and freedom. We

Holding six-week-old Basil, the first baby Not Forgotten Ministries' helped save

had a team of nineteen volunteers, offered post-abortive Bible studies in two different counties and online, and we were offering miscarriage support groups as well as infertility support groups. An ultrasound machine had also just been delivered, which would enable us to offer a free ultrasound to every woman entering the abortion clinic.

How did all of this happen? Why would God allow me to be a part of something so amazing? Considering all God had done in just one year caused my heart to overflow with gratitude.

My Reflections

There were times in my past when I felt as if God had forgotten me or even hated me. There were times I felt completely alone and rejected by the people who should have loved me most. There were times when I questioned every circumstance I endured and whether I had any value at all. When I look back over my past now, especially since I had the abortion in 1999, I clearly see how God was steering me back toward Himself and His plan for me. Every single thing I endured had a purpose and was used for good in my life.

Although continual rejection and abandonment had adversely affected my view of myself and altered my sense of value, it eventually helped me to let go of my obsession with the opinion of others. I began to to follow God even when it made no sense to those around me.

Having a miscarriage was not something I deserved, or a punishment given by God. It was an opportunity for me to grasp how precious life is. With that experience I felt tremendous loss even though I was only several weeks along in my pregnancy. That caused me to better understand what I had done with my first pregnancy.

Being injured at work and struggling with pain for so many years was a difficult situation brought about through evil in this world, but God transformed it into a gift that allowed me to be in the right place when God called me to homeschool my kids. The worker's comp settlement helped us get the home we needed for our growing family. I also wouldn't have met Melissa, the friend who shared her abortion story, or had the flexibility in my schedule to begin the ministry, if I had been working.

Experiencing the shocking birth of baby boy number three wasn't God's way of laughing at me. It was His way of teaching me, in a very personal way, how intimately He knows each one of us, even when no one else does. I learned more about Him and my own identity through that experience than I could have any other way. I also began to grasp how well He knew the child I aborted, even while she was in my womb.

Being diagnosed with an awful auto-immune disorder was not a punishment by God, although I do believe it was a ploy of the enemy to try and incapacitate me. Instead of God healing me miraculously, the way he healed my back, He is continually showing me His strength in my weakness. He is helping me to depend fully on Him. My children are also learning empathy and compassion for others through my pain, which is a beautiful gift. Additionally, even though I have this terrible disease, He is *still* using me- which proves He can use anyone, at any time, regardless of anything we might see as a hinderance.

I've spent a lot of time looking back through my past, and after allowing God to speak over the various seasons I've endured, I now see the purpose in the pain. Just like me, everyone has ups and downs, ins and outs, and junk that doesn't make any sense. We are often so quick to run away from our past, try to hide from it, ignore it, and even wear a mask to keep the world from seeing what we've experienced. But we can only run and hide and ignore for so long. Eventually, if we want to move forward with God, we must go back. We need to acknowledge the different seasons of our lives and allow God to reveal the ways He was steering us and guiding us all along. Confronting pain instead of running from it is unnatural. Being transparent instead of hiding isn't easy. Purposefully learning from the past is hard work. Looking back is both beautiful and painful simultaneously but doing this will cause us to develop some appreciation for the areas of our lives that we've wanted to cover up. We will observe that our Heavenly Father is the God of the mountain and of the valley. And in doing so, we will begin to clearly see how God used even those things we wanted to hide to slowly sanctify us.

God is in the business of completely rearranging the makeup of our mistakes. What we consider shameful, He uses for His glory. What we want to hide, He wants to expose so that others may know they are not alone. When we feel disqualified, weak, or abandoned, He strengthens, equips, and walks beside us. For me, He took the one thing I desperately tried to hide for seventeen years, He stripped it of all its power over my life, and began using it to save the lives of babies and Mommas from the pain and heartache of abortion. He made my past, my purpose.

Photography by Jennifer Howard Photography

Epilogue

As I HAVE OPENED my heart and recorded my thoughts on the pages of this book, I have seen afresh God's relentless pursual and continual involvement in every detail of my life. I am in awe of His goodness. Bryan and I have been married for sixteen years now and we still live in the white house beside the pond. We are like a new couple in many ways, falling more in love all the time. Our children are twelve, eight, five, and three years old. They bring me joy and laughter every day. My relationships with all my parents are the best they've ever been, and they are my biggest cheerleaders as I move forward in the fight against abortion. I spend my days homeschooling my children and leading the pro-love, pro-life ministry God has given me. Life is good because God is good.

My Family, April 2020.
Photography by
Jennifer Howard Photography

My dad, me, and Allison

My brother, me, my mom, and my stepdad

I'm under no illusions, however, that life will always be perfect or that all my difficult days are behind me. But I move forward on this journey clinging to John 16:33, where Jesus said, "In this world you will have trouble. But take heart, I have overcome the world." Jesus has already won. I do not need to live in fear or consider myself a victim. What others think of me no longer matters because my identity is rooted in the One who created me. He who is in me is greater than he who is in the world (1 John 4:4), so I can walk in confidence and authority because He has given me the victory.

I've come to realize that Jesus didn't give His life as a sacrifice just to get us into Heaven. He gave His life in order to get Heaven inside of us, which results in the abundant life He desires for each of us. When we decide to trust the Holy Spirit, even with the ugliest parts of our lives, it's as if we are taking the limits off Him. Our surrender allows Him to lead the way and the journey is better than we could ever imagine.

**Allison wearing the dress I
bought in Africa 20 years ago**

Slaying giants, walking on water, healing the sick, and raising dead bones to life are not just the miracles of the Bible. Even if it takes decades, God will wait patiently on His children and when we're willing, He'll use us in miraculous ways.

He built me for this battle, and He has incredible things in store for me. The same is true for you.

FOR MORE INFORMATION ABOUT abortion, to contact Tori, or to participate in a post-abortive Bible study, please visit www.theyarenotforgotten.com or send an email to theyarenotforgotten@yahoo.com